Stay, D

Request · Read · Return

...Your Library. Delivered.

Published by the Perera-Hussein Publishing House, 2020
www.pererahussein.com

ISBN: 978-955-8897-32-4

First edition

Stay, Daughter is a personal memoir. The right of Yasmin Azad
to be identified as the author of this work has been asserted by her
in accordance with the Copyright, Designs & Patents Act.

Excerpts from the memoir have been previously published as:
Swimsuit, in the Spring 2017 issue of *Solstice Literary Magazine,* (USA).
Food-Wrapping, in the Spring 2019 issue of *The Massachusetts Review,* (USA).

Printed and bound by Thomson Press.

 To offset the environmental pollution caused by printing books,
the Perera-Hussein Publishing House grows trees in Puttalam –
Sri Lanka's semi-arid zone.

Stay, Daughter

Yasmin Azad

PERERA-HUSSEIN PUBLISHING HOUSE
COLOMBO

If you want to understand today,
you have to search yesterday

For my beloved sons
Kalid, Siraj and Jehan
And for my nephews and nieces
Rashid, Ayesha, Naima, Laila and Amal

With much affection

PROLOGUE

*And stay in your houses, and do not display
yourselves.*

—The Quran

We did not stay in our houses. Not in the way our grandmothers had, or our mothers. We went out a little more and veiled ourselves a little less.

Casting off the heavy black cloaks that had once shrouded females from head to toe, we covered ourselves, instead, in flimsy veils. Draped lightly around our heads, the silks and voiles fell casually from our shoulders, and in the minutes it took for us to get from front door to car, a stranger walking on the road could make out the features of our young faces, the curves of slender waists and hips. Sometimes, such a stranger fixed his eyes on us. And sometimes we looked back. Mothers drew our veils closer and hurried us away; you shouldn't allow yourselves to be seen like that, they told us.

Like girls from infidel families, we went to school, and stayed there even after we had become "big." And still more like them, but so unlike our mothers, some of us longed for more learning and dreamed about leaving home to get it. The elders shook their heads and cautioned: too much education could ruin a girl's future.

The world outside was pressing in on us, and when I turned twelve, Wappah, thought it time to tell me a story. Many years ago, my father reported, when our country, the island of Ceylon, was still a British colony, an Englishman—perhaps the Governor himself—had invited a Muslim statesman to dinner. "Bring your wife too," the important official said. "I have never met her."

"Aaah," came the reply. "That is not possible. She is in purdah and cannot be seen by men outside the family. But," the Muslim man continued, as he pulled out a rose from a nearby vase, "look at this. It would be just like looking at her."

My father beamed and nodded as he ended his story. I looked back and said nothing.

If we felt the stirring of wishes unknown to our mothers and grandmothers, we didn't tell them. They would have been shocked, like Wappah, who had only known women like flowers.

1

Men are the protectors and maintainers of women.

– The Quran, 4:34

ot three years after she had become a bride, Wappumma, my father's mother, became a widow.

"She went into shock when they brought the news to her," Aunt Asiyatha said. "Rolled on the floor and wailed. What was she going to do? Your grandfather had died in Bombay on the ship bringing him back from Mecca. 'Who will guard us now, who will guard us?' your Wappumma kept asking. She was six months pregnant too. Lost the baby."

Aunt Asiyatha was my father's cousin—the adopted daughter of his mother's only brother. When, as a girl, I accompanied Wappah to his childhood home in the village of Shollai where his sister still lived, she was often there. Patting down a straw mat spread on the floor, my aunt would say, "Come sit here; I have some things to tell you." I would sidle right up. As far back as I can recall, I latched on to anyone who would tell me a story.

Aunt Asiyatha spat out a stream of dark red betel juice and continued. "What was your Wappumma going to do? Your father was a toddler, and his sister only a little older than that. Who was going to look after them?"

"Didn't Grandfather have money?" I asked.

"Yes, but he had all those children from his first marriage. He couldn't leave everything to your grandmother. Soon, the money was used up, then the jewelry was sold, and all the plates and most of the furniture, and in a few years, there was nothing left."

"Didn't they own land?"

"All that came to nothing. The paddy field in Weeraketiya, she used to get a bag of rice once or twice a year, but the rest of the properties, nobody knows what happened to them."

"What do you mean, no one knows what happened to them?"

Aunt Asiyatha leaned over and lowered her voice. "Don't tell your father I told you, you know how he is when anyone speaks badly of his relations, but they say a man, one of our relatives, he brought your Wappumma all kinds of papers, got her to rub ink on her thumb and put it down, and one by one the properties were gone. We think they were sold off."

"But what was written on those papers?"

"Allah, child, how would your grandmother have known?"

My father's mother could not read or write. She couldn't tell time or make out a calendar. She needed help counting money.

"When were you born, Wappumma?" I once asked her.

"When was I born? My mother told me it was during Uncle Omar's wedding. Cousin Fathuma was just learning the *aleph, bey, thay* of the Quran, and her little brother had begun to eat solid food. That's when I was born."

"No, which year? How old are you?"

Wappumma knitted her brow and shook her head.

My grandmother's life kept rhythm with the moon; she kept track of its waxing and waning. Every four weeks or so, when it seemed about time, she stepped out into the garden and searched the night sky. If she spotted what she was looking for—the faintest of crescents glowing in the dark— she hurried to announce that a new month had begun. Her days began when the stars came out; she said her Friday prayers on Thursday night.

Though she fathomed little about things outside her home, Wappumma was convinced she understood the workings of the world. Someone envious had cast the spell that had taken her husband and comfortable life away. How else could it all have ended like that? But she protected her family now. She hung amulets on her son and daughter—sachets of magical charms tied with thick black string and secured around arms and necks and waists. They warded off the evil eye and the evil tongue, and the many other evil vapors the whole village knew were waiting to enter the unsuspecting orifices of children. She said special prayers at nighttime, too, to keep away the demon jinns.

Once, she found a pumpkin in her backyard that no one could account for. Who had thrown it there? Maybe that same evil person who had cast the first spell. Had she been a fool and cut the fruit open, streams of blood would have come pouring out and put a hex on everything in the house. She yelled out a curse and threw the jinxed fruit over the fence. She was too clever for her enemies.

When I was about eight, Wappumma placed an amulet around me too, but my mother took it off. Umma said that it was mostly people in the villages who wore such things. She didn't add that people in a town like her home of the Galle Fort, where we now lived, never descended to such behavior, but I sensed that was what she meant, and in that case, I was happy to take it off.

When her husband died, somewhere around 1910, the colonial officials representing His Majesty in the district of Galle requested that my grandmother submit last wills, affidavits, and properly notarized deeds. The Registrar of Births, Deaths and Marriages, of whose existence she had barely been aware, demanded to know the *exact* dates of events. Wappumma looked to a man in her family, someone who knew the ways of the white people, to stand in her stead at the courts and registries. Perhaps, it was he who had brought those documents and said, "Put your thumbprint down here."

Aunt Asiyatha tucked a fresh wad of betel leaves into her mouth and fixed her eyes on my father who was sprawled on a recliner on the other side of the back verandah, chomping on his cigar.

"He it was, who guarded them. Your grandmother, she always said, 'my little Abdul Rahuman, after he began to work, we never stretched out our hands to anyone.'"

My father's sister, whom I called Marmee, brought out cups of cardamom-flavored tea and joined the conversation. "Thambi was so small when he went to work, half a sarong would cover him from waist to ankle. Our Umma would cut one into two and hem the edges. That way, he had one piece to wear while the other was in the wash."

Wappah pitched his voice across the room, as his ears had picked up the familiar name for little brother, *thambi*. "I always woke up at dawn. As soon as the muezzin at the mosque called out the morning prayer, I jumped up from my mat."

"Nice jumping up from the mat!" Marmee laughed. "I shook his shoulders, and shouted into his ears and splashed water on his face, but he just pulled his sarong over his head and rolled over. Then Umma put her head into the room and yelled. 'Only a boy visited by Shaitan would sleep until the sun shone on his behind!' That's when he got up."

"As though the sun could have shone on my behind or anywhere else in that dark corner of the floor where I slept!" Wappah scoffed. "But I didn't say that to my mother. Would have got a good slap on my face if I had."

"That's right," Marmee lowered her voice. "In those days, he was not a *periyal*, a boss. He had to listen to *us*. We told him what to eat and when to go to sleep and made him take his baths. And that...*Subhanallah*!" My aunt shook her head and raised her eyes and hands upwards.

Wappah, Marmee said, would run all over the house and garden to escape a bath at the backyard well. He crept under coconut fronds, squeezed his scrawny frame behind the outhouse, climbed into empty gunnysacks. His mother always found him. Her hand curled tight around his bony wrist, she would drag him across the yard, over drying jak leaves, goat droppings and chicken feathers, and set him down on a slimy patch of ground by the dugout well where his sister waited—a bucket of water drawn and ready.

When the first chilly cascade landed on his head, he sputtered and hopped from foot to foot. His teeth chattered. He snorted water out of his nose and shook it out of his ears. Before he could catch his breath, another torrent of cold water hit his shoulders. Then, another and another.

"Scrub all the dirt out, or he will get sores again!" Wappumma shouted from across the yard where she squatted over an open hearth, making breakfast.

Marmee would wedge a sliver of yellow soap into a piece of coconut husk and scrub: neck and back, arms and shoulders, down the legs and the spaces between the toes. When the next bucket of water landed, it fell on skin scraped red. Her brother screamed.

"When Thambi got his first job," Marmee smiled, "he started to take good baths on his own. He knew he had to look good to work in a place like the Galle Fort."

A relative who knew of Wappumma's descent into poverty had secured for her young son a job as apprentice to a jeweler in the Galle Fort, a fortress in the southwest corner of Ceylon. This had been the military stronghold of European colonizers for many centuries. Built by the Portuguese in 1588, some decades later, it was wrested away by an invading Dutch army. Finally, in 1796, it came into the possession of the British, the last of the Westerners to rule the island. By the early twentieth century, when my father was a boy, the Fort was no longer an army garrison. It had become the administrative and commercial capital of the Southern province. A thriving citadel with hotels, warehouses, shops, schools and churches, it was also home to civilians, several of whom — and this was of utmost importance to Wappah and everyone in his village — were some of the most prestigious Muslims in the country.

When her brother set off in the morning, Marmee stood behind the front window to watch him leave. He was eleven or twelve (no one in the village knew exactly when they were born) when he first began to work, and she being about two years older, was, by this time, a "big girl" who had been brought inside. To keep herself unseen by strange men, she did not set foot outside her home during the day. As a *komaru* — a female past puberty but not yet married — the rules of seclusion were far stricter for her than even for her widowed mother.

Pressed against the wall and leaning in against the wooden frame of a little window, Marmee got as good a view as she could of the road beyond. A little while ago, her mother had made breakfast. Squatting over the open hearth, she had swirled a batter of flour and coconut milk in a sizzling pan, and made hot, crisp rice wafers. The smells wafted in and mingled with the odor of damp walls, dirt floors, and goat droppings that always hung in the air of the little house.

Outside, the dew was wet on the grass and the only people to be seen were the men in white tunics and caps who were returning from dawn prayers at the mosque. Marmee's eyes followed her young brother as he walked along a footpath that led away from clusters of small houses built with bamboo and clay. She saw him swipe a juicy guava from a neighbor's garden and tuck it into the knot of his sarong. The ground was cool to the soles of his bare feet but soon the sun would rise, and before he reached the Fort, more than two miles away, beads of sweat would glisten on his forehead. A few feet ahead, beyond a grove of coconut trees, was Talapitiya Road, the main highway that cut through the village of Shollai. There, he took an abrupt turn and vanished from sight.

"I waited all day for him to return," Marmee said. "When it was time to light the oil lamp at dusk, I went back to the front window and looked out."

Leaning in against the wall again, and peering out through the wooden bars, she caught sight of the coconut palms that threw long shadows on the grass. The same men and boys in white tunics and caps who had been out in the morning were now on their way to the mosque for evening Maghreb prayers. They walked by the house without making out any part of her, not at all suspecting that a pair of girlish eyes was gazing out into the world.

Her brother came into view as he turned the corner from the main road — a small figure lugging a basket of fish and vegetables, veering from side to side to avoid the piles of cow dung that dotted the field. When he approached the front steps, Marmee called out to her mother, and Wappumma hurried to take down the crossbar that had been set against the front door. It had been there since her son left in the morning to shut out anyone or anything that could intrude on the modesty of the widow and her daughter.

"Don't let any outsiders in before you have given us time to hide," Wappumma always told her son as he stepped inside. Now that he was home, neighborhood boys and male cousins several times removed might walk into the house. He didn't need the warning. Early on, he had acquired the trait that was to last a lifetime — the fierce protection of female honor. Acutely aware of the presence in his home of the *non-mahram* — the unpermitted male — he allowed no man in before he had shouted out a warning and heard the patter of feminine feet hurrying away.

The first sign of such a man approaching, and Marmee fled. She didn't linger a second longer than she should have. Or so she told me. She appeared to be one of those girls, so numerous in those days, who if their elders drew a line on the ground and said, *don't put your foot beyond this, not even one little bit*, they never did. I didn't ask Marmee whether she was ever a bit curious about which man or boy was coming into the house. The question would have flustered her. It wasn't something she allowed herself to think about: that she could choose to look or not. Her life was what it was supposed to be, nothing more or less. This was the key to the unquestioning obedience always held up for those of us who were showing signs of being less than perfectly docile. Besides, one of the lines drawn inside my own head, which I did not easily cross, was the one that said, *don't ask unnecessary questions*.

No sooner than he had stepped inside, Marmee eagerly asked her brother what he might have seen in the Galle Fort that day. He brought reports of buildings three and four times as tall as their house, verandahs enclosed with rows of glass windows, and gates of polished brass you could mistake for gold. She tried to imagine what a motorcar looked like, marveled that white ladies walked all on their own in broad daylight, and that children were taken around in wheeled carriages. The day she heard about water that had turned into cold blocks of stone covered in sawdust, and sold by a man who pushed a cart, she wondered whether her brother made things up.

Marmee was most impatient to know about the happenings in the homes of the wealthy *shangakara* Muslims in the Galle Fort. To be told about their large houses with ornate gables, tiled roofs, spacious courtyards, and name boards with English lettering: *Ocean View, Eglington, Jasmine Cottage, Haley;* the ebony divans and elaborately carved tables set up in the front halls; the tall ceramic vases and dwarf palms along the inner courtyards. And how intricately carved and beautiful the wooden lattice screens were, without exception, that sealed off the women's quarters.

Her brother described what he saw as he walked by the double Dutch doors that opened out onto wide verandahs. What lay within he didn't know. He never stepped inside any of those stately homes. In those early days, Kuhaffa Hadjiar's jewelry shop on Leyn Baan Street was the only smooth floor in the Galle Fort that took the imprint of his dusty feet.

Before Marmee was done with her questions, her mother waved her aside. The widow had waited all day too, for her son to come home.

"A jackfruit fell down in the front garden. Pick it up before someone else does…Walk to cousin Zubeida's house and tell her I'll come by to see her after dark…I've been waiting to drink something. Can you pluck a King coconut for me?"

Wappah was happy to oblige—he didn't want his mother to go outside her home more than absolutely necessary. They may have been poor, but he wasn't going to allow people to say the females in his family roamed the village like infidel women.

His presence at home was valued most, at least by Marmee, when the roving salesman, Majeed Nana, came to the village. This itinerant trader carried on his head, a huge cloth bundle packed tight with textiles and fancy goods. His appearance always thrilled the maidens of Shollai who never set foot in a shop themselves.

A few weeks before the great festival of Ramazan, wives, daughters, sisters and aunts would divulge their preferences to the men in the families who did the shopping for them.

Some men ignored these declared choices and bought what *they* thought would look good on their female relatives; others, returning home with arms full of packages, learned to their befuddlement that taffeta was not the same as satin, and that silk came in various grades and textures, not all of them equally desirable. A few particularly sharp fathers and brothers *did* know how to choose "a saree with threadwork along the edges but nothing on the front border and no sequins unless they were the kind that wouldn't come off if a small child was to tug on the fabric."

Lately, some fashionable Fort ladies had begun to ask that they be taken to the entrance of textile stores in the Galle bazaar. Seated safely inside their curtained buggy carts, they chose from bolts of fabric that were brought to them. Marmee found it hard to believe that women could be so forward.

She gave no instructions, either, to her brother, so she said. And whatever Wappah brought her was alright, she said too. Yet, she counted the days till it was time for Majeed Nana to visit the village.

On one such day, Marmee, when she was fifteen or so, heard a loud voice.

Sarongs! Sarees! Cloth!
Sarongs! Sarees! Cloth!

She searched for her brother. Where was he? Had he stepped out into the backyard or gone to look for their roaming goats? Was he in the outhouse? She had no time to lose. If no voice stopped him—and only a male voice could do that—the trader would walk right by their house.

Wappah had heard Majeed Nana too and came running. When he called out, the cloth trader stopped and turned, then with slow steps, walked up to the small house. At the front door, he propped a wooden yardstick under the bundle on his head, shifted it to his shoulder and carefully brought it to the ground.

"*Salaam alaikum, salaam alaikum*," Majeed Nana said aloud, as he wiped his forehead with the back of his hand. He pitched his greeting into the air as though he was speaking to no one in particular. But he knew full well, that watching his every move through a crack in the doorway, holding their breath until he untied his package, were the women of the household. The older, married females holding the door ajar, and the *komarus* standing behind, peering over their shoulders.

"Shiny satin…Manipuri sarees…Chintz…India muslin…Java sarongs…" Majeed Nana described his merchandise aloud as he laid them one by one on a white cloth. "Why," he exclaimed, in a voice that was carried into the house, "this is what you get in all the fancy stores. If truth be told," he pitched his voice a little higher, "this is what the Fort ladies like."

The cottons came first: the cambric and flowered chintzes women used for everyday wear, the striped Java sarongs worn by men. Next lace, both broad and narrow, for trimming blouses and underskirts. And last of all, the sarees: delicate voiles, Manipuri silks with intricate cord work, georgettes embroidered in every color of the rainbow. When Majeed Nana wiped his hands on his sarong and unfolded the yards of an embossed chiffon, Marmee gave a little gasp.

She had no place to wear such a saree. Besides, they could not afford it. But Wappah brought it in for her to see.

"Take your time, take your time," the trader said, speaking into the air once again. He was an unhurried man, well used to sitting on his haunches on some front verandah, while men and boys carried his merchandise in and out. Women rubbed their cheeks against soft silks and murmured. They draped liquid folds over their shoulders, ran their fingers over delicate embroidery, held shiny fabrics up to the sun, and chose what to keep and what to give back.

After the textiles had been displayed, Majeed Nana took up the tin box that had been at the very top of his bundle. Inside, in a tray divided into compartments, were coral beads, perfumed soaps, and talcum powder. He set all that aside and reached for the container at the very bottom. Marmee tightened her hold on her mother's arm.

Nestling in folds of white voile were dozens of glass bangles: red, blue, green, yellow, even gold; some multicolored, some striped diagonally over the narrow bands, others with shiny specks inside the glass. They glinted in the light. With just two bangles on her wrist, a girl could make a delicate, tinkling sound.

Marmee turned to her mother.

Wappumma shook her head. "The glass will break when you do your housework; and where else could you wear them? Where do you go child, that anyone would see?"

Marmee bit her lip and said nothing.

But Wappah walked up to Majeed Nana's box and picked up a pair of bangles. He said if it made his sister happy, he would buy them for her.

The next morning, after her son had left the house, the widowed mother placed the crossbar against the front door and closed it shut.

2

Let not the believers take the disbelievers as Friends.
– The Quran, 3:28

ecause it was the custom among our people that when a man married he moved into his wife's home, our family lived in the Galle Fort, where Umma had been born.

After some years as a jeweler's apprentice, Wappah had struck out on his own and become wealthy enough to be considered an eligible bridegroom for a daughter of the prestigious Cassim clan, to which Umma belonged. Marriages like that took place when a Fort family could find no one amongst themselves for a girl who was unmarried and growing old. No one ever explained why Umma, who everyone considered beautiful and elegant, had not been able to marry earlier. I couldn't really ask, that being another unnecessary question, but I suspect it had something to do with the decline of family fortunes—the decline that often happened to the subsequent generations of wealthy families. Where no big dowries could be offered, people who were otherwise keen to be set apart from those who lived in the villages allowed themselves to consider an up-and-coming bachelor from a place like Shollai.

The Galle Fort, this place where I grew up, was like no other. Or so the *Ulemas*, the religious scholars of Islam, must have concluded with great consternation. They insisted the faithful keep away from the infidel; inside this cramped citadel, no one could keep very much away from anybody else.

Perched on a cliff that jutted out into the sea, the fortress was a small outcrop of land surrounded on three sides by water. Inside, within an area that was less than a tenth of a square mile, lived hundreds of people. With roofs and gutters touching, and only a common wall in between, their houses jostled against each other. To talk to a neighbor, a person stood in his courtyard and shouted over a wall, or sat on the steps of the front verandah and pitched his voice across.

The back doors opened out to narrow alleyways, giving cover to Muslim women who wanted to visit their relatives without walking the streets. They also opened out to minuscule pieces of land that families used for raising livestock. Here, a neighbor's goat wandered over to chew on sprigs of jak leaves brought from the countryside, and a neighbor's ducks waddled in to splash in mud puddles left behind by monsoon rains. The smells from adjoining kitchens mingled and wafted in the breeze and into this mix was added, every day, another odor, when the bucket man from the municipality opened a latched door at the back, and emptied into his handcart the brimming pails that he pulled out from the latrines.

My mother's uncle, Zain Magdon insisted that the first Muslim allowed to live inside this citadel was one of our own ancestors. Nearly two centuries ago, his great-great grandmother, Raheema Umma, a widow with seven daughters (all of them very beautiful, Zain Marma also insisted), had lived in Magalle, a small town a few miles south of the Fort. Some hooligans who knew about the pretty girls began to harass the family, and one night, the notorious bandit Kitchel, who worked with the fearsome robber Gurubaldi (so Zain Marma's story went), broke into the house to abduct them. Though the cries of the women brought out the neighbors and the widow and her daughters were saved, the next morning, the terrified mother appealed to the colonial authorities to give her a safe place to live.

At the time, there was a Dutch law that restricted Muslims—whom the colonizers called Moors—to their own enclaves in the country, but in 1774, Raheema Umma was allowed to move to the safety of the Fort with its army barracks and impregnable walls.

Not everyone in the Fort was willing to accept that it was someone in Uncle Zain's family who had been the first to move there—such distinctions were only grudgingly conceded. But when challenged, Uncle Zain whipped out the evidence: Dutch Governor Willem Jacob Van der Graff's census of 1789 *did* have an entry for a Moor widow with seven daughters living in the Fort; and the name of the widow *was* recorded as Raheema Umma.

When this great-grandmother, several times removed, first settled into a house on Church Cross Street, she lived, a lone Muslim, among Christian Burghers—the middle-class traders from Holland whom the Dutch had encouraged to migrate to their Asian colonies. After the British repealed, in 1832, the law that restricted the rights of the Moors to live where they wanted, more of them migrated into the Galle Fort. Traders by profession, they appreciated the advantages of living near what was then the country's principal harbor. Eventually, a large community of Muslims came to live inside this fortress, among the descendants of the white-skinned people who had colonized Ceylon. We called them *Parangis*, from the Arabic *Ferengi* for Frankish crusaders.

"Grandfather Rohani Cassim spent so much time with the Parangis," Kaneema Marmee told me, "people began to talk."

Kaneema Marmee was the oldest of a group of relatives who regularly got together to chat over afternoon tea. The daughter of my mother's paternal aunt, Thalha, she was Umma's first cousin. Nearly every day, they gathered at our house on Lighthouse Street in the Galle Fort, to sit by our spacious courtyard and be cooled by the gentle sea breeze. The savory pastries and sweet confections our cook laid out, made it even more of a favorite venue.

"What were they saying about your grandfather?" I asked Kaneema Marmee. Someone had lain themselves open to almost the very worst thing that could happen to a person—have people *talk* about them. Someone in my own family, no less. Had this person not cared? I felt a thrilling shudder just considering the possibility of such boldness.

"They complained that he was spending too much time with the *Marshazi*."

The Marshazi were 'others'—*maru* in Tamil, meaning different and *shazi* meaning group, or type. The Parangis who were Christian naturally fell into that group. They were people unlike us— infidels from whom, the Ulemas warned, we were to stay away.

"Didn't other people do that?" I searched my aunt's face as she took a bite from a crisp pastry.

"Not the way *he* did."

Great-grandfather Rohani Cassim, I learned, was not like most other Muslim men of his time who worked as local tradesmen dealing in gems, hardware and cloth. He was a ship chandler who sold coal, oil, rope and other supplies to the foreign vessels that berthed in Galle. In the middle of the nineteenth century, when he began his business, this harbor in the south of the island was a port of call for hundreds of steamers, mail boats, and military vessels. Travelers from all over the world disembarked from visiting ships, and with a regularity its residents came to expect, the narrow streets of the Fort teemed with Europeans in white morning dress. Many of them, directly or indirectly, were Rohani Cassim's customers.

His exposure to the ways of the Marshazi must have been more than for most, which was saying something, since there was hardly anyone among the faithful in this fortress who was shielded from the unbeliever. On the verandahs of spacious houses were men who smoked and drank alcohol. Everywhere were unveiled women who walked the streets by themselves and stopped to talk to strangers. At celebrations in the fancy hotels were the couples who danced to music.

The believers were tempted even more directly. Such were the activities the Parangis had introduced. During horseracing season, for instance, who could resist standing on the tall batteries of the Fort to watch the stallions who galloped to a finish on the esplanade below? How many Muslim men must have gone into the betting stalls to engage in the prohibited pastime of gambling?

Even the pious who stayed away from such haram activities were becoming more familiar and at ease with the ways of the foreigner. On their way back from afternoon prayers, if they took the road around the ramparts near the mosque, they would see the heads of colonial agency houses, in short trousers and knee socks, swinging golf clubs and shouting into the wind. Perhaps one or two among the believers not only stopped to watch this unusual game but also chased after wayward balls and threw them back.

Great-grandfather Cassim was someone who was likely to do that, having become, as people were beginning to notice, very comfortable hobnobbing with the Parangis. Needing to talk to ship captains, he had learned enough of their foreign languages to communicate with them; this of course allowed him to strike up conversations with other Marshazis who came his way. He likely became an acquaintance of the Dutch Burgher Henry Andre, who had established a mail service from Galle to the capital city of Colombo, and perhaps also Mr. Janz, who was the manager at the booking office. They must have chatted while they waited, weekday afternoons on Custom Street, for the mail coach to come rattling over the drawbridge of the old moat.

"The way Grandfather became friendly with the Marshazi—that was too much," Kaneema Marmee said as she picked up the conversation again. "At least, that was the complaint."

I was about nine when I first heard this story, and for some years now, Umma had let me play with and spend long hours at the house of my Christian classmate Penny.

"How friendly are we allowed to be?" I asked.

"The Ulemas say we can be good neighbors and do business, but we shouldn't become very close."

"What's 'very close'?"

"Taking them to our hearts."

I didn't know at the time what exactly it was to take somebody to my heart, but I imagined that what I was doing with Penny—giggling nonstop, holding hands when we walked, and telling her all my secrets—probably came close.

"Why? What's wrong with that?"

My aunt took a while to answer. "Well, the Ulemas say that's how you begin to pick up their bad behaviors."

As far as I could tell, my behavior with Penny was not that much different from my behavior when with my Muslim playmates. But with grown-ups, you could never tell. I was at an age when I was beginning to realize that they could find fault with you for going against rules you didn't even know about.

Kaneema Marmee looked into the distance before she brought her attention back to me. "People said it was because he got so friendly with the Marshazi, especially that Mr De Vos... his neighbor—you know the house?'

I nodded. Everyone knew the prominent Dutch Burgher family.

"Because old Mr De Vos became Grandfather's friend, they said—that's why he did what he did."

"What? What did he do?" I nearly knocked over the tea tray, and Umma, who was busy with her sewing on the other side of the room, looked up.

"Came home one day and announced he was going to send his daughters to school."

3

To imitate the Infidel is to become them.

– Hadith, Abu Dawood

In 1963, in the town of Buraydah in Saudi Arabia, men rioted when the first girls' school was opened. King Feisal had to send the National Guard. For a year, the only student was the headmistress' daughter.

– Geraldine Brooks, *Nine Parts of Desire*

Perhaps it was a balmy day in 1887 when Great-grandfather Rohani Cassim held his six-year-old daughter, Thalha (Kaneema Marmee's mother), by the hand and walked her out of the house and down stretches of open road, to the English Girls' School on Middle Street. It was the kind of thing you could expect, the shocked people of the Galle Fort said, from a man who made friends with the infidels. Of what use was the reading and writing of foreign languages? Why sully the minds of his children with knowledge of ungodly people and places? Hardly anyone thought it necessary to educate even their sons beyond what was needed for writing receipts and keeping accounts in a shop, and here was a man ready to send his daughters to school. A school run by Christian missionaries no less.

"Did Great-grandmother object?" I asked Kaneema Marmee, "was *she* willing to send her daughters to school?"

Kaneema Marmee considered this question about her mother's mother. "I don't know for sure. But her father had been an interpreter for the Dutch, so he must have mingled with the Parangis too. He changed his name, you know, from Makhdoom to Magdon to make it sound more like a white person's name. He probably liked the Marshazi too."

"He didn't think of sending his daughter to school, though?"

"Nooo, not during your great-grandmother's time, over a hundred years ago. There wasn't even a girls' school in the Fort."

My mother's family, I was being told, had a penchant for mingling with the infidels. Perhaps that's why—and I made this connection only much later—Umma let me spend so much time at Penny's house. When Umma's lawyer uncle Zain, who everyone snickered had "really taken the Marshazi to heart," sent his youngest son Usuf to play with Penny, I was allowed to tag along. Soon, I was spending whole days with her and even sleeping over during weekends.

I didn't reveal this last fact to Kaneema Marmee. I thought it might be a bit too much, even for someone from the Cassim family. I had overheard disapproving comments about Umma having a soft spot for certain Marshazi ways, and I really didn't want people to *talk* about my family, or me.

So, as Kaneema Marmee described it, her mother, my Grandaunt Thalha Cassim, continued to walk to school even as men on the road stopped and stared, and women standing behind lattice screens flapped their hands. Her father had not cared. Not only did she go to school, but when their time came, all of her younger sisters enrolled there too—to sit next to infidel classmates and learn their lessons from foreign teachers.

No matter how much they enjoyed learning, each of Great-grandfather's daughters, when she turned nine or ten, was pulled out of school. It was unthinkable that a girl would go out of her house when she was close to puberty. If their father had considered it—and knowing his stubborn ways, people speculated he might have—their mother probably put some sense into him. "Who would come looking to our family for brides, if after they had grown up, the girls were seen running around a school yard with their heads unveiled and their legs below their uniforms shamelessly bare?"

❀ ❀ ❀

My Grandaunts having all gone to school, I discovered, was connected to a routine that my mother established in our home.

Umma wanted all the newspaper food wrappings that came to our house. Not the smallest pieces scrunched around a handful of betel nuts or sugar crystals, but anything bigger than a note page. Full sheets of newsprint were best, but these had sometimes been folded over a pound of tuna or mackerel, and smelled of fish. They were thrown away, of course, but not, I recall, before they had been held up over the trash bin and a glance or two taken at the blood-soaked pages. Through the day, our maid stacked the torn-out paper in a corner of the whatnot in the dining room. At tea time, Umma dragged the canopy table to the edge of the courtyard where the sun streamed in, smoothed out the creases with her tapered fingers, and leaned over to read.

Umma could read when most other women her age could not, because of the tradition in her family that girls get at least some education. But because it was also the expectation that they would be taken out from school at age nine or ten, she had dropped out after third grade.

"I would have cried and rolled on the floor," I told Umma, "if that had happened to me."

"Why would you have needed to do that?"

"Because it's school. I wouldn't have wanted to leave."

"Everyone left early in those days."

"But I would have asked Wappah to let me stay. Couldn't you have asked your Wappah to let you stay—just a few more years? If you had cried and cried and said you wanted to, he would have let you. I think he would have."

Umma shook her head. "I didn't think anything about it. All the girls left school after third grade." She picked up her sewing and thrust her needle into the fabric.

I brought up the subject again a few days later. Leaning against her sewing chair, I asked, "But if someone really, really liked school, Umma? You should let them stay, shouldn't you?"

Umma snipped off the end of her thread.

"What do you mean—stay in school? Most girls stay now, till at least the eighth grade. Mostly tenth."

"But, some girls…"

"Some girls?"

"Well… some girls, they study for a long time, right up to the end of school and even after that."

"Not *our* girls, they don't. You know that, right?" Umma searched my face. "Right?"

I looked back and said nothing.

I wondered what my mother did during the long days at home after she had left school. We had no storybooks in our houses—only the Quran and prayer missals. Hardly anyone in our families sang or made music or painted. It wasn't the kind of thing the Ulemas encouraged. Sometimes women played a drum at weddings. But how long can you play a drum by itself? And how many weddings can there be? Maybe that's why Umma had become so good at sewing.

"Didn't it make you sad when you had to stay at home all day? Junoodha Marmee told me she cried when her younger sister went off to school and she had to stay back."

"No. I got used to it. People get used to things. They always do."

We got used to it. Everyone in the older generation said that. It was the explanation for everything that had happened in the past. The reason for keeping everything the same in the present. The comfort that would eventually come in every hard situation. I never heard anyone wonder whether there were people who couldn't get used to things. And what would have to be done about them.

It was some time before I spoke again. "But you had nothing to read. No story books or picture books or anything!"

"I did read."

"Read what?"

"I read the newspapers—all the food wrappings that came to the house. There were all kinds of tories there, news about accidents on the road, people who had been robbed and what was happening in England—when Princess Elizabeth and Princess Margaret Rose had been riding their ponies. Things like that." Umma smiled.

"Really?"

"Yes. The difficult words, I would ask my Wappah or my brothers."

I moved closer to Umma as she talked.

"The double sheets were the best. I waited and waited for them. You could get a complete story there. The small pieces were sometimes torn right in the middle of the most interesting part."

"Then what did you do?"

"I kept looking in the next day's wrapping or the next."

"Did they ever come?"

"I don't remember that it did."

If the printed word came to her, Umma seized it. Every morning, when the paperboy on his bicycle balanced one foot on our doorstep and sent The *Daily News* sliding over our cement floors, she hurried to pick it up. She read it through from top to bottom, all the pages, except the sports section at the back. Any news about the royal family in England, she eagerly lapped up. Her lips tightened if the fashion pages displayed scanty clothing, and the *Bringing up Father* comic strip made her laugh as loudly as she ever allowed herself to. "That Maggie, using a rolling pin to hit her husband. Imagine!"

Umma picked up the printed word in other places too: a newspaper that someone left behind on a train (trains and not buses being the only public transport that was considered suitable for the Muslim women of her generation); magazines in a doctor's office; some stray reading matter at Zain Marma's, one of the few houses among our relatives with books lying around.

Once, she asked to go back to the dentist though he was done working on her teeth.

"But he said you needn't come back!"

"I know. But I didn't get to finish the story in the *Femina* magazine that was in the waiting room."

"Umma, we can get *Femina* delivered to the house. Would you like that?"

"No."

"It's easy. We just place an order at Lake House bookshop and the postman will bring it."

Umma shook her head.

"But you don't have to do anything at all."

"No," she said in a firm voice. "That's not what I am used to."

Of the new-fangled notion taking hold in the Galle Fort of allowing girls to go to school, a dowager of my grandmother's generation had this to say: "It will give them *ideas*, you wait and see. All this reading and writing. They will neglect their household duties and turn away from prayer. They may even—" and here, the old lady had drawn her veil closer and lowered her voice— "stuff love letters into mango seeds and throw them over the back wall. Then what will we do!"

Mothers and fathers ignored the warning. Sometime after Great-grandfather Cassim had sent his daughters out of the house to get an education, other families followed suit. By 1937, forty-three Muslim girls had been enrolled at the English Girls' School, and by the 1950s when I was growing up, not only did almost every girl go to school, she stayed there until at least the eighth grade.

The first to do that, as might have been expected, were my mother's cousins, the daughters of Thalha Marmee—that girl from the Rohani Cassim family whose going out of the house had shocked everybody in the Galle Fort so many years ago. Thalha Marmee's oldest daughter Kaneema, though she got more schooling than her mother, had dropped out relatively early. But the younger girls in the family had stayed on. Haleema not only went to school after she had become a "big girl," but also set her sights beyond reading and writing. She acted in plays, performed in concerts and led the patrols of her Girl Guides troupe. Then she passed the Junior Cambridge Examination. Her little sister Fathuma followed in her footsteps. Two young maidens, going out of their home at fourteen, unveiled and in short dresses. *Fourteen*, when a girl was almost a woman.

It came in very useful for Umma and her other female relatives that their cousin Fathuma had acquired all that education. Her knowing English and the ways of the white people helped with those things they couldn't negotiate themselves. If a child brought home a report card that said she needed to be more *diligent*, Fathuma Aunty, as I called her, could explain that it meant she needed to work harder; if someone was described as not being *punctual*, that meant they were often late. When a recipe created in England called for *dripping* to be melted in a pan, you had to use animal fat.

Just being around Fathuma Aunty expanded Umma's vocabulary: the plural of *Madam*, she knew, was *Mesdames;* the glass jug on the bedside table, everybody was informed, was properly called a *decanter*. And if people were going to indulge in the disgusting native habit of chewing betel, this Junior Cambridge qualified lady insisted, they had better use *a spittoon*.

Fathuma Aunty wrote her own letters too, without badgering her children to do that for her, like other mothers. *Thanks ever so much for your kind letter recently received*, she often began, and when she signed off, she sent everyone her best compliments.

And all her female relatives Fathuma Aunty judged by a single, unyielding standard: *can she read a jam label?*

Umma asked Fathuma Aunty to take me to places where it helped to know the language of the Marshazi really well. So it was that my aunt took me to Mrs. Bartlett, the Burgher dressmaker on Middle Street, whose skills even Umma, who was an excellent seamstress herself, held in awe. No one could match Mrs. Bartlett in making replicas of the outfits that appeared in *Weldon's Fashions for All*, the English magazine Galle Fort women passed around before Ramazan.

"My mother, you know, *never* went to places like this when she was young," Fathuma Aunty told me as she held my hand and walked up the steps to the dressmaker's house.

This was true. By the 1950s and early 60s, much had changed in the Galle Fort. Hardly anyone now wore the full burkha when they stepped out of their homes. There were even some women, if people could believe it, who hardly bothered to cover their heads at all. A woman would still never sit in the front seat of a car, not even if the driver was her husband or son. But the days of automobiles curtained at the back to seclude female passengers were fast receding. No one would ever mistake a Muslim woman for a Parangi. Not yet. Her dress and manners would immediately identify her as vastly different. Yet, some deep-rooted changes were setting in, and it was perhaps recognizing the threat of the slippery slope that had made some of the traditionally faithful react as they did to what was going on in Rohani Cassim's home.

"They threw stones at the house," Kaneema Marmee said.

"People threw stones at your mother's house?" I asked.

"Yes."

"Why?"

"They were angry."

"About girls going to school?"

"That too, probably. But what they said was, they were angry about the piano."

"The piano?"

When little Thalha Cassim and her sisters went to school, Miss Lucy Vanderstraaten, their teacher in kindergarten, had not only taught them to read, but also to clap hands to "Ring a Ring of Roses," "Here We Go Round the Mulberry Bush," and "London Bridge is Falling Down." And the little girls, enthralled by the sounds that tinkled out of the big wooden box with ivory keys, asked their father to get them a piano.

This caused a problem since some Ulemas had said music is haram. Even those who concluded that it was permitted didn't think of it as anything to be encouraged. It was the kind of activity that seduced people into dancing and drinking and all manner of bad behavior; one thing could lead to another and you couldn't predict where it would all end up.

Music in the Galle Fort certainly came from the Marshazi, not anyone else. Every Sunday, from the Dutch Presbyterian Kirk on Upper Church Street and All Saints on Middle, bells pealed and hymns spilled out into the streets. Alongside the harbor, the grand bands of visiting ships regularly played dance music while crowds stood by to listen. The most religious of the infidels' songs came too, once a year to people's very doorsteps. On Christmas Eve, Portuguese carolers dressed in colorful clothes walked the streets and stopped every few yards to sing. While violins played, the young among the spectators intertwined their arms and danced on the streets. Muslim men stood on the verandahs to watch, while their women peered from behind wooden screens.

Perhaps, on such nights, Great-grandfather Cassim carried his daughters out front so that they could lean over the verandah wall and look at the man who turned the *Nathal* lantern around and around, spinning the images of the Virgin Mary, Baby Jesus and the Star of Bethlehem. Perhaps the little girls got on the floor and twirled right along to these seductive sounds.

"The sounds, that's what they said bothered them," Kaneema Marmee nodded. "The piano distracted the pious on their way to the mosque."

"But the house is so big. You almost can't hear from one end to another! How could it disturb anyone?" Here again was the uneasiness that had been aroused in me: even when you didn't think you were doing anything wrong at all, it was possible to get into trouble. What were the rules, and even more, who had the right to make them?

Kaneema Marmee paused. "We were called the Parangi *koottam*, the Parangi clan. People complained that our women crossed their legs when they sat and carried handbags like nurse ladies. That the men had become London *kungees*, London brats. But the reason they threw rocks was the music. So they said."

The changes that were overcoming the community would eventually have happened with or without the prompting of the Parangi *koottam*. Hardly anyone who lived in the cities and towns in twentieth century Ceylon was able to resist, or even wanted to, the forces of westernization. There were too many social advantages to becoming modern.

For the Muslim women of the Galle Fort, perhaps it was advice from their prophet himself that was hastening change. He had insisted, and not once but many times, that we treat our neighbors well. A generous family—and generosity was a cornerstone of the faith—during Ramazan, shared with the Christians next door a mutton biryani topped with fried raisins and cashews. At Christmas, they received in return a cake decorated in delicate pink roses, frosted over with crystalized sugar. In the inner rooms of her home, a girl said: *I'd like to learn how to make icing flowers just like that*, and a mother or father, seeing the longing in a daughter's eyes, decided it was not so outrageous that she would go to a Parangi lady's house to learn this exquisite art—wasn't she going out of her home anyway, when she went to school?

There were many advantages, even for girls, to learning the language and adopting the manners of those who ruled the country. All over Ceylon, privileged children were wearing western clothes and speaking English, and the Galle Fort Muslims did not want to be further behind the times than was absolutely required by the rules of the religion.

Our girls could not, like their brothers, go away from home for higher studies, or hobnob with the ruling elite by playing tennis at a Gymkhana Club—that was going too far. But they could take on some Western fashions and manners, and they did. They wore knee-length frocks and court shoes with heels. No longer did they wait patiently while their mothers oiled their hair and combed out the tangles in long black strands. They cut their hair short, stood before mirrors and patted a fashionable *bob* into place. Under their sarees, women wore a *chemise*, and their little daughters, under their dresses, bloomers trimmed in Nottingham lace.

Families in the Fort who had once arranged their days around the rhythms of the Islamic year began to keep track of a child's birthday on the English calendar and celebrated it, too, with a ribbon cake made by the Burgher Miss Jacotin. Soon, a girl was considered a desirable daughter-in-law *only* if she could make such a cake herself, and only if she could sew a tailored dress after the fashion worn by Parangi children.

Chaperoned maidens in the Galle Fort veiled their heads, walked the back alleyways and dashed across ten feet of road to places where someone would teach them how to make marzipan violets and sew Little Lord Fauntleroy suits, complete with lace collars and knee-breeches. A little Muslim girl setting out on Ramazan day, fitted in a frock that Mrs. Bartlett had made, with an "Alice band" on her head and Clark's buttoned shoes on her feet, could almost be mistaken for an English child — which was the whole point of being taken to the Parangi dressmaker's house that her grandmother would never have considered entering.

Because Umma had little experience with the institutions that had become part of her children's lives, she took Fathuma Aunty along when she needed to talk to the Irish nuns at my school, Sacred Heart Convent. Watching Fathuma Aunty among these white people, I thought she looked more like them than like us. With her very light skin, short hair and lips colored red, she could have been mistaken for the lady in the advertisements for Pears Transparent Soap.

Like the Parangi ladies in the Galle Fort, Fathuma Aunty played "A Maiden's Prayer" on the piano, and, like them too, hung paintings on her walls. She had done that in the 1930s and 40s when no one else had considered such a thing. This was partly because such decorations were an unknown, foreign custom, but also because people took seriously the preaching of the Ulemas, who had said no one would be tormented in hell more than the painters of images. Fathuma Aunty obviously disregarded their warnings: *The Blue Boy*, in his satin jacket and trousers, with one hand at his waist and the other holding a feathered hat, looked out into the world from above her sideboard.

Like foreign ladies, Fathuma Aunty called her husband by his given name, which, as any elder among our people would have explained, was not the thing to do. Not at all. The name of someone so revered was not to be bandied about, and when a properly respectful wife wanted attention, she was supposed to say, "Look here," or "Listen," or

"Are you there?" In his absence, she could refer to her spouse as "The house person," or "The children's father," or just "Him."

Years ago, women whose husbands were away or dead would come to Great-grandfather Magdon-Ismail, who was a Justice of the Peace, to ask for help with legal matters. As they stood modestly behind a screen to answer his questions, an inevitable one would come up.

"What is your husband's name?"

"His...name?" the woman would stammer.

"Yes, his name."

She looked to someone who could answer that question and if no such person was available, went back home only to return with a child in tow. Taking her position behind the screen once again, she instructed a young son or daughter, "Tell the gentleman your father's name."

"Zain!" Fathuma Aunty called out to her husband. "Zain!" No matter how many times they had heard it, Umma and her cousins whipped their heads around. When she walked breezily into a room, crossed her legs on the divan and asked, "So how are your *hubbies*?" they probably choked on their tea.

Nobody threw rocks at Fathuma Aunty's house as they had done at her mother's. It had become more acceptable to not hold so rigidly the lines that divided the Marshazi from us. And, in any case, how much could anybody control from outside those boundaries between *them* and *us* that people might have crossed in the recesses of their minds? All I knew was that if I had to spend time at a relative's (and the Ulemas said it was always good to spend time with your relatives), I finagled a visit to Fathuma Aunty's. I hankered after the books and pictures she owned that had come from across the seas—that seemed the principal enticement. Or so I thought. Looking back, I realize that what drew me most strongly was being around someone who had made an inner journey to a place far from where she had been born, and didn't seem to much care who knew about that.

4

What leads to the forbidden is also forbidden.

— Principle of Sharia law as expounded by Imam Malik

esides the time I spent at Penny's house, my most frequent dealings with the Marshazi happened at Sacred Heart Convent, a girls' school established by Irish missionaries. Situated a little outside the Fort, it was the educational institution of choice for middle class Muslim girls in Galle. And almost from the first day I set foot in this place full of people *unlike us*, I had questions.

Was a nun a girl or a boy? That's what I wanted to know when I was in first grade. Sister Bernadette wore a dress, which was like a girl. But her hair—I saw through a gap in her bonnet— was short and stubbly, and that was like a boy. So which was it? It was no use asking Wappah, he said he knew nothing at all about the people in my English school. So I asked Penny and she said nuns were girls, definitely.

From Penny, I also learned about the pictures that hung in the classrooms and hallways. The baby in the box of hay? That was Jesus—his mother and father were too poor to get him a proper bed. The man in a brown robe with a sparrow perched on his shoulder? He was St. Francis—who loved birds and animals. Why were there so many pictures of a heart covered in thorns and blood? That was how our school got its name—it was the Sacred Heart of Jesus. When Penny wasn't around, I tried to figure out a story myself.

I shared her Sunday school books. In *The Illustrated Children's Bible*, I discovered Jonah who had gotten himself swallowed by a whale, Pontius Pilate who was a very bad man, and Moses who went down a river in a basket. Soon, I knew exactly how to fill in the coloring pages: the shepherds' robes in stripes of brown and yellow; the plumes on the Roman soldiers' hats, in the deepest, darkest red.

There were no pictures in the madrassa where I learned Islamic religion. On Saturdays, during *Ahadiya* lessons, we sat on wooden benches and shouted out the answers when Razik Nana, our teacher, asked his questions.

Who are we?

We are Muslims.

What is our religion?

Our religion is Islam.

Our voices reached the rafters and bounced off the walls, white and bare except for the splotches where the paint had started to crumble.

Razik Nana continued:

Who is our prophet?

He is Muhammad, peace be on him.
Who is his mother?
Armina, peace be on her.

There were no statues or pictures in the Galle Fort mosque either. Being a girl, I had never been inside, but once, when I balanced my toes on the parapet wall surrounding the outer garden and peered inside, I saw there was nothing except prayer mats: no statues or pictures or decorated glass windows. A single bare lamp hung from a chain in the ceiling and swayed from side to side when a breeze blew through the wide arches.

One day, in madrassa, Razik Nana told us how, when the prophet was saying his prayers in a cave, the angel Jibreel came down from Heaven to give him the Quran.

I knew that angel. Penny had called him Gabriel in the picture where he wore a long white dress, had wings, and a golden circle over his head. He was telling the lady in blue that she was going to have a baby. I wanted to jump up and tell Razik Nana that I knew all about the angel. But if I had, Razik Nana would have swung his cane in mid-air and made it come down on the table with a "thwack!"

"Haram!" he would have said. "It is *forbidden* to draw pictures. *Forbidden*! Angels do not come into houses where there are images. Do not look at such haram things."

But I did want a closer look at images I only glimpsed from afar. Umma had said I could go anywhere with Penny, except to a church, where, the Ulemas warned, people prayed to false gods. Penny had said that the chapel where the nuns prayed was not *exactly* a church, and seeing no reason to question her too closely, I promised to help with her arithmetic homework if she would sneak me in.

There was very little light and at first all I could dimly see were colored glass windows, flickering candles, and shiny brass bowls. Up front was a statue of the lady in blue with her arms outstretched and, by a door that led out of the room, a picture of Jesus—he had that golden circle around his head. The large painting showed him with a stick in one hand and a lamb in the other. All around him were groups of sheep, some munching grass, some looking into the distance, and others with their heads turned towards him. They wanted him to look at them, I thought, but he was smiling down at the lamb he held in his arms.

"That's the Good Shepherd," Penny explained. The lamb had run away and got lost and Jesus brought him back. Right there, I thought, was a fine story. The lamb running away, Jesus looking all around, perhaps spotting him behind a bush somewhere, and chasing him down, his robe flapping in the wind, maybe those thick sandals tripping over cobblestones. "No! No! No!" Penny said. "That's not it! Jesus loves the lost lambs best, that's what the picture is about."

For weeks after, I tossed that picture around in my head. What did it mean to love the lost lambs best? There was no one else I could ask without letting people know I was taking an interest in the images of a kafir religion. So I figured something out on my own. I decided if I were a lamb, I would run away and get lost every chance I got. There was no point to sticking around and being ignored.

Far different from this educational institution full of Irish nuns was Wappah's childhood home in Shollai where I often spent Sunday afternoons. Wappah thought it a good day for me to visit his sister where she lived, in their old home with her husband and children. Wappumma was there too until she passed away, when I was about ten years old. My three older brothers Naufel, Sheriff and Bunchy hardly ever came because no one seemed to expect that boys would take time off to make family visits. Besides, they did not have much in common with Marmee's only son, who didn't go to the same school or spend time with the same friends. My aunt's three daughters did not have much in common with me either, but Wappah said I should stay close to them, no matter what.

He never, as far as I knew, asked Umma to come along. Fort ladies who had married outsiders from the towns and villages beyond, generally preferred the company of their own relatives and made only the most perfunctory visits to their in-laws. Ever since Umma, as a bride, had seen Wappumma wipe the rim of a coffee cup with the edge of a saree that had been worn all day, she made any excuse she could not to go to Shollai.

Sunday being the driver's day off, my father, who had learned to drive late and never took the car out unless he had to, would prepare to get behind the wheel. First, he tightened the belt over his sarong. Then he shook out his handkerchief and cleaned his glasses. Lastly, he slipped off his sandals and put them on the passenger side—he was more comfortable using his bare feet on the pedals—and settled himself behind the steering wheel of our Austin A40.

Our garage, like others in the Galle Fort, was narrow, and the road outside barely ten feet wide. When Wappah lowered the rearview mirror, turned the key, shifted the gear into reverse, and inched out, one wall or the other was usually in the way. He drove back in. Then he turned the wheel all the way around, craned his neck and went back out again. On a rare day, he was able to get the car out on his second try; more often, it took a third or fourth. While he went back and forth, I coughed from the petrol fumes, and our houseboy shouted directions over the roar of the engine.

"Keep straight, you'll hit the door! No, no, a little to the right!"

"How much to the right? Don't say a little."

"I don't know, just a little."

"You didn't warn me about the pillar!"

"I didn't see it!"

"Move over to the other side. Move over and tell me how much room there is."

Soon, a group of bystanders, of whom there never was a shortage in the Galle Fort, joined in.

"More to the right!"

"Cut left! Cut left!"

Beads of sweat collected on Wappah's forehead. He looked one way and then the other, gripped the steering wheel with both his hands and shouted in his gravelly voice.

"You fellows keep quiet! I know what I am doing!"

Sometimes, a wheel fell into the storm drain and a loud, collective "Aiyooh!" burst out. That was the signal for the houseboys loitering at the Lighthouse Street junction to leap into action. "Come, come," they hollered, as they tightened their sarongs and ran up. "We have to get P.T. mahathaya's car out of the drain."

One Sunday afternoon, when I was about eight, a day when I had even more reason to want to set off without much delay, we did. Ten minutes after Wappah had got into the car, it was out of the garage, facing the right direction, and on its way to Shollai.

We made our way down Lighthouse Street, past the tennis courts of the Galle Gymkhana Club, and out from under the main Fort gate. People who knew us smiled and waved, but Wappah gripped the steering wheel and looked straight ahead. Soon, we were driving by the esplanade where boys played cricket in their blinding white shirts and caps, their arms wheeling above their heads. Across from that field of close-cropped grass was the *Pacha Gaha*, the "liar's tree" where street hawkers sold medicinal oil they said could cure every illness and amulets they swore could ward off every evil. Wappah never drove by the *Pacha Gaha* without a long tirade: "Just because everybody believes something doesn't mean you should too. Fake healers, bogus holy men, and greedy politicians. Liars all." He slowed down to take a look at these particular set of fraudsters.

"Let's go, Wappah, let's go quickly," I said.

At last, we turned into the main street of the Galle bazaar. I rolled the window down and put my head out. It was coming up now, on the right side of the road between a dry goods shop and a bakery: W.M.M. Salies Hardware Stores.

Nearly everyone had an interest in Salies Hardware in the Galle bazaar. Women bought their kerosene cookers from there, men dropped by for flashlight batteries, and school children came for fountain pens. For some time now, when we drove to Shollai, I'd had my eyes on what leaned against the bi-fold doors at the entrance: a bicycle with the cross bar angled down, steel spokes glinting, and red and blue plastic ribbons fluttering from its handlebars.

"Can I have a bicycle, Wappah?" I asked as we neared the store.

"A bicycle? Why do you want a bicycle?"

"For riding around."

"For riding around? What? Girls don't ride bicycles."

"My friend Penny does."

"The teacher's daughter?"

"Yes."

"She's a Parangi, that's different. Our girls don't do such things."

"But I'd like to. I would really like to."

"No...everybody will say you are behaving like a boy."

People raised their eyebrows at *ambula kadijas*, tomboys, and disapproved of anything that blurred the line setting girls apart from boys. When our drill teacher at school asked us to wear divided skirts, the Muslim mothers wrung their hands—the girls would be wearing clothing separated in the middle, like trousers. Some came up with a design of pleats that went over the waist so that, though it was divided, the uniform looked just like a regular skirt. Umma got me exactly what the teachers asked for because she had respect for schoolteachers and said we should do what they wanted us to. She didn't care as much as everybody else, I also suspected, about girls looking like boys.

"Please, Wappah. I told Penny I would get a bike," I held the back of the driver's seat.

"Why did you tell her that without asking me?" Wappah's voice was sharp.

I didn't say anything in reply as it dawned on me that I had to be careful about blurting out what it was I did with Penny.

Wappah looked at me through the rear-view mirror. "Don't I get you all the dolls you want?"

This was true, he did. My toy cupboard was full of beige cellulite figures that had once dangled from the rafters in the Galle bazaar. We usually got them on our way to Shollai. I had fancy walkie-talkies too from Colombo. "You spoil her," Umma sometimes complained when Wappah handed over yet another doll dressed in an organza dress, with a bow in her hair. But when I buried my face in a mass of golden curls or breathed in the fresh smell of new porcelain, he smiled and said, "I like to make her happy."

We were getting closer to Shollai when Wappah spoke again.

"You can't do everything the Parangi girl does."

"Aiyo! Wappah!"

"Do any of your cousin-sisters ride bikes?"

"No."

"See? That's what I mean. There are things that girls do, and things that boys do, and they are not the same."

"But…"

"No. You know how Umma tells you don't whistle or laugh out loud like a rowdy person? Riding bikes is like that, not proper."

I moved into a corner of the back seat.

Wappah fixed his eyes on the road ahead, and for some time there was only the sound of engine and wheels.

"You would really like a bike?" he suddenly asked.

"Yes!" I sat up and leaned forward.

Wappah looked back at me again. "Well…I'll think…no, no, I'll bring you a doll from Colombo. A very nice doll."

As it often happened, my father changed his mind and I eventually got my bicycle. Red and white, with gleaming steel spokes and handles, it had the word *Raleigh* written on the bar that angled down. Wappah took me to Hayley's in Colombo to pick it out. He said we could get a better one there than in the Galle bazaar.

I had told him again and again how much I wanted a bicycle and explained what a good thing it would be for me to be able to ride everywhere with Penny instead of being left behind, and promised to be a good girl and fast all thirty days of the month of Ramazan. Wappah tweaked my nose and said, alright, he would get a bike since I was still a little girl, but warned me that I was not to dress like a Parangi, in those short trousers.

I tried my best with the fasting and didn't eat or drink a drop of water from sunrise to sunset even though the fasting month that year, when I was nine years old, had come during the school term and in the hot season, and a girl had fainted one afternoon, inside a classroom. Only on one scorching day, I came home from school feeling like I was going to die of thirst, and when no one was looking, gulped down a whole glass of the iced coffee that was supposed to be for later in the evening. I told myself that was alright, because sometimes the month of Ramazan, if someone spotted the new moon right away, had only twenty-nine days, not thirty, and so when I fasted for twenty-nine days, it could be considered a whole month, couldn't it?

With a bike that was my own, I went to Penny's house. On weekdays after school, I gobbled a raisin bun, gulped down a glass of milk, and told my ayah who looked after me where I was headed. Umma, at that time of day, was just waking up from her afternoon nap. If she saw me, she would tell me to sit down and read some of the Quran before I went anywhere. As quietly as I could, I wheeled my bike past her room, waited on the front verandah for the road to clear, and dashed off. If I went early enough, Penny would still be doing her homework and I would get a chance to read her books before we took off for the ramparts.

I possessed few books; none at all like those that filled a cupboard in Penny's bedroom. Penny's mother bought them for her all the time, but it was I, not Penny, who rummaged the shelves that burst with stories of animals in top hats and short trousers, toys that sprang to life at night, a house deep in the forest made of gingerbread, and girls and boys who solved the mysteries of pirate caves and abandoned farms. I stood on tiptoe to reach the highest shelf where *The Children's Classics* were lined up; I peered into the back where little triangles of dust had settled into the corners. When I found a book I wanted, I walked out to the courtyard. If it was new, I brought it up to my face and breathed in the smell of fresh paper and print. Then, I sat on the cool cement floor next to a pot of red anthurium lilies, arranged my dress around me and with my heart beating a little faster, turned the first page.

When we eventually ran off to the ramparts to play, my head full of the stories I had read, I told Penny we should try to have adventures. She didn't see how; the Bobbsey Twins and the Famous Five lived in America and England where such things were more likely to happen—the only places, we had reason to conclude, where anything happened that was worth writing about. But, I pointed out, the Galle Fort could be an exception. With its ruined lighthouse, spooky closed-up buildings, massive ramparts, and shallow coves, we had as good a chance as any of spying on smugglers and tracking down thieves. And it wasn't as though we didn't try. We watched for suspicious activities on Bathiri Cove, the shallow inlet where we bathed; we stood atop the stone steps leading to the dungeons near the clock tower—we were too afraid to go inside; everyone knew that the Dutch had chained their captives here—and looked for signs of ghosts, though we didn't know what that would be, in the middle of the day. We formed a secret society too, and had our meetings on the grassy circle of the old lighthouse, surrounded by its broken walls. I made badges that said *SS*, and chose a password that I changed every month after I learned that was how it was supposed to be done.

The treasure maps we drew led to the places in the Fort where we weren't allowed to go: the new lighthouse where a board said everybody had to keep out, the old Flagstaff where it said the same thing, and the ledges below the steepest and most dangerous of the ramparts, which we couldn't even approach without some adult throwing a fit. Penny said that she didn't see the point; we didn't know of any treasure to be found. I told her we didn't know for sure, but one of our maps *could* lead to a chest filled with gold coins. Penny's mother, whom I called Aunty June, smiled when she saw my maps—she often organized treasure hunts for birthday parties. Umma raised her eyebrows though, which was only to be expected since she had never read a mystery story in her life.

When we were not trying to have adventures, Penny and I rode our bikes up and down and around and around the winding streets of the Fort. Our hair blowing in the breeze, our arms and legs outstretched, we took jumps off the slopes of the rampart greens and laughed hysterically as we fell down on the grass that cushioned our knees and elbows.

5

Iqra!

– The Quran, 96:1

"Read!" was the first word of Revelation.

Taking stock of the inordinate time I spent not doing what I was supposed to, Umma complained: "Soon all the people in the Galle Fort will know," she said, "that you cannot even recite one verse of the Quran, properly. And other girls your age know whole chapters. What are you going to do about that?"

What I was doing was sitting way in the back during group prayers, ensconced in the folds of some Aunty's saree, moving my lips in pretend recitation, hoping no one would call on me to chant *anything*. Hardly anyone did. Girls in the Fort had the same teacher and word got around.

My mother rarely organized *mowloods*—group prayers—at our house. This trait did not win her many friends, considering, people said, that she lived in one of the bigger houses in the Fort, where a hundred women could comfortably sit. Instead, in a quiet spot in the house, she veiled her head, lit a single joss stick and took the holy book onto her lap. Smoothing the white satin of the dust cloth, she ran her fingers through the silk threads of the tassels, and if I hadn't been able to slip away, corralled me. "Come sit here. If you listen while I recite, you'll learn something."

When Nueman Lebbe, my Quran teacher, walked into the house at three-thirty on a weekday afternoon, I dragged myself from whatever it was that I was doing and looked for my Arabic primer. It could be under a pile of toys, fallen behind the divan, or mixed up with last week's newspaper. I searched for my headscarf, went to the bathroom, and drank a last glass of water. Nueman Lebbe tapped his fingers on the dining table and waited.

"Have you reviewed your lesson?" he asked when, at last, I sat down.

"Yes," I lied and opened my book. "*Bismillahirrahumaniraheem*, in the name of Allah, the most merciful, the most beneficent!" I said that first line of every prayer in my loudest voice. Nueman Lebbe was not impressed.

Placing my forefinger under the lines on the page, I stumbled along. Was that letter a *sin* or a *shin*, an *ayn* or a *ghayn*? Some parts of the alphabet I knew; with others, I made wild guesses. This was not a language I spoke—we spoke Tamil among ourselves, and Sinhalese, the majority language of the country, with nearly everyone else. A tiny group of the westernized spoke English as well. But no one, unless they were the religious Ulema, understood Arabic—I was learning only to sound out words. I shifted in my chair and looked again at the page: rows of dots and dashes, scallops and waves; black lines on tissue-thin paper. Nueman Lebbe took out a bottle from his pocket, spilled a dab of fine brown powder into his palm and inhaled. When he dusted his hands and sent a thin film of brown powder into the air, I coughed for far longer than I needed to.

Nueman Lebbe was like an Ulema, except less learned. He had studied Arabic at a college like the one on Church Street where lived dozens of religious students who walked the streets of the Fort all the time. I usually crossed to the other side when I saw a Lebbe. Once, though, I came up close to the head teacher of the Arabic College. I was riding my bike on the ramparts when he came walking down the street, leading a group of students. Dressed in white tunics that fell below their knees and white sarongs that stopped several inches above their ankles—that was how the prophet had worn his cloak, several inches above the ground—the young men walked with their eyes fixed on the road. Just as I rode down a grassy slope and landed on the road, they reached a spot ahead of me. I put both feet on the ground. The head Lebbe raised his head and frowned.

Did he know who I was? Probably not. I never went to the mosque. We never had mowlood gatherings at our house where he might have seen me, and I had not made any kind of name for myself in religion class that he could have heard about.

The Lebbe continued to glare at me from underneath thick eyebrows. Could he tell that I sneaked away from Arabic lessons? That the only reason I knew even one verse was because Umma made me say it every night? He probably thought I was an infidel. I had all the signs: my hair was cut short, my dress reached only to my knees, and my legs were astride a bicycle. Or did he look at me like that because I was a girl? I could not tell. A faint scent of musk floated into the air. With my eyes lowered, I wheeled my bike to the edge of the street and rode away.

If I could have learned Arabic without too much effort, I would have. It would have been very nice to have people pat me on the head and say *Do you know she is only ten years old and has memorized 15 verses?* Or however many verses it took to get that kind of praise. But I would have liked the compliments to rain down without much effort on my part. I had other books I wanted to read.

And those, besides at Penny's house, I found at the Tamil man's secondhand bookshop on Pedlar Street. The Tamil man, who everyone said was a *Kalla Thoni* — an illegal boat person from South India — lived in a garage that backed into an alley. In a corner of this dark room was his 'shop' — rows of cardboard boxes overflowing with old copies of *Time*, *Life*, *FilmFare*, and, stacked on the floor, piles of comics he sold for five cents each.

Tarzan, *Superman*, *Donald Duck*, *Mickey Mouse*, *Archie*, *Little Lulu*, unwieldy towers leaned against the back wall, the covers torn, and the pages limp from the moist air that was everywhere in the Galle Fort. To get to them, I had to walk around a threadbare camp cot and under a rope on which was hung unwashed sarongs and undershirts.

Wappah would have bought me books if he had known how. I gave him a list before he left for Colombo every Wednesday—*color pencils, bubel gum, bangels, hair slides*. When he returned on Saturday, they were usually in his bag. Once, I asked for "balay slippers" after I had read about Margot Fonteyn in one of Penny's *Girl's Own Annuals*. He brought me a pair of pointy-toed boy's shoes—the shop boy had roamed all around town and it was the closest thing he could find. Had I written, *a storybook I haven't read before*, Wappah would not have known what to do with that.

The Tamil man sat by the open storm drain and chewed on a wad of betel leaves. I rummaged through a pile of comics, fitting torn pages together and flicking away silverfish. When the front cover was whole, it was a story in itself: *Scrooge Leads His Nephews On a Slickery, Trickery Trail to Find the Jillion-Dollar Diamond*. On the back, it was usually Charles Atlas promising an Atlas body in just seven days.

Comics explained life in America: boys who liked algebra and wore glasses could not find girlfriends; you could tell right away when someone was stupid—their front teeth jutted out; the fair-haired man was the good guy; bad guys had dark hair and thin mustaches.

Some things, though, I wondered about. Why did children need babysitters? Where were their grandmothers, aunts and older cousins? How could Jughead raid the fridge at midnight for leftovers? Wouldn't his mother have given all the food away to the poor people in the neighborhood? When Little Lulu said a cheery "Hello," to Mr. Jones, her neighbor, and went off to fight the boys, her mother didn't say, a) *you must wait for the elders to address you first*, and b) *don't fight, girls shouldn't do that*. When Archie looked at Miss Grundy straight in the eye and protested, "I failed the test? There must be a mistake!" he wasn't asked if *that's how he respected his teachers*. Girls met boys at the soda fountain and no one gasped, *what kind of a shameless thing is that?*

The Tamil man spat out a stream of betel juice and muttered, "Buy the books you want, don't read them here." I stood up and noticed for the first time the rows of mosquito bites, like tiny pebbles, down my arms and legs. Dropping some coins into the shopkeeper's outstretched hand, I hopped on my bicycle and rode off.

Nueman Lebbe drummed the table again; I turned another page and faltered along. The minutes passed. In the still quiet of the afternoon, the wall clock ticked loudly. With my chin propped on my hand, my eyes drifted off to a spot on the far wall and stayed there, for how long, I don't know. I looked up just in time to see Nueman Lebbe's fingers curled around his ruler, the three hairs on his knuckles each standing on its own black dot of skin. "Whack!" His ruler came down hard on the table. With a start, I dragged my thoughts away from pirate treasure and farmhouses with cobwebs on the windowpanes.

Not talking too much about the books I read or what I did at Penny's turned out to be the best thing to do. It saved me from Wappah ever finding out that I had seen *Swan Lake*.

Aunty June often took me to see the English films that were showing at the Queen's Cinema. I saw Mario Lanza in *Seven Hills of Rome*, Leslie Caron in *Gigi* and Yul Brynner in *The King and I*. Wappah had tried a few English films himself. "All they do is talk, talk, talk," he said. No heroine with jasmine garlands wound in her hair who twirled the end of her saree as she ran down a hill; no hero with dazzling white teeth and a thin black mustache who sang sad love songs and fought the bad people at least three times in one film. "You go see all the English films you want," Wappah tweaked my nose. "I'm going to see Sarojini Devi and Sivaji Ganesan in *Paalum Palamum*."

The only film Umma had ever wanted to see was *The Ten Commandments*. She said it was worthwhile because it told the story of the prophet Musa who was sent down the river in a basket and found by the pharaoh's daughter. The immensely wealthy Mubarak Hadjiar obviously thought so too. He bought out the entire matinee showing at the Majestic Theater in Colombo so that a dozen of his female relatives could see the film without having to sit next to men not related to them.

I never asked Aunty June what we were going to see. Penny and I were thrilled to just be in the theater, knocking our knees in the dark as we groped for our seats, giggling at everything, and eating icy-chock popsicles during the interval.

When Uncle Quintus, Penny's father, turned his car into the parking lot of the Queen's, I saw the huge billboard: a ballerina standing on her toes, her head bent down and arms folded over her chest. Across the top, the words *Swan Lake* were written in big black letters. I could hardly wait to get inside.

The film began with velvet curtains opening out on a stage. As an orchestra played, a dancer twirled, raised her arms above her head, and lifted a leg high above the floor. A troupe of swans in white tiptoed around her. Some time later, a male dancer bounded in. He leapt from one end of the stage to the other and spread his legs wide. Above his waist, he wore a short black jacket embroidered in silver, and below it nothing at all but white stockings. Fitting tight, the thin cloth stretched over his lower body, ankles and calves, knees and legs, and most prominently, the bulge between his thighs. I heard a gasp from behind. "Aiyo! What kind of indecency is this?" Someone exclaimed in Sinhalese, "*Vili lajaavak!*" Unthinkable shamelessness!

While the ballerinas continued to twirl and dance, and the male dancer spread his legs and leapt, the people behind us got up from their seats and walked out. I looked over to Aunty June. She had her eyes fixed on the screen.

What would Wappah say if he knew that I had watched men prancing around without proper clothing? He might wonder what else I did at Penny's house that he didn't know about—which wasn't a lot, but was not exactly nothing either. After Penny showed me how to dance the Twist to Chubby Checker's music, I practiced the steps at home: one foot grinding the floor, hips swinging from side to side. My brother, Sheriff Nana, saw me do that and laughed. But he didn't report it—we children who went to Christian schools and had infidel friends had an unspoken understanding that much in our lives had to be hidden from our parents. When I wanted to try on Penny's white shorts with the tabs and bronze buttons I smuggled them into my bedroom. Umma had said I absolutely could not wear Parangi clothes like that and I never intended to wear them outside the house anyway. Someone might see me and say *shameless*. They would talk about me. In addition, if they reported it to Wappah, he would have called me a bad girl. Now what would he say about *Swan Lake*? No more English films; maybe no more playing with Penny. My mouth went dry.

I looked around the darkened theater. There were very few people. That was usually the way with the films that Aunty June took us to. And coming in, I hadn't seen anyone I knew. So who was going to tell Wappah that I had seen a dirty film? Not me, I decided, as I settled back in my chair to enjoy it to the end.

But try as I might, it was hard to keep secrets in the Galle Fort. This, I realized, when Ameena Thatha who lived on Leyn Baan Street called me over one day. She thought it her duty to say something to me.

"You spend a lot of time in that Parangi house, no?" she asked.

I was walking to the ramparts and Ameena Thatha was with her sister, leaning over the wall of the front verandah, as many women did at that time of the afternoon, to watch the traffic go by. She was not a close relative, and had hardly ever spoken to me before.

"Yes," I said softly.

"Do you spend the whole day there?"

"Sometimes."

"And sleep at night?"

I nodded.

"Why does your mother let you do that?"

I hesitated. "I like to play with Penny."

"Can't you play with your Muslim friends?"

I crushed the gravel under my shoe. I did play with my Muslim friends, but what I came across at Penny's, I didn't find anywhere else. But to tell her that and talk back to older people was unthinkable. Besides, would Ameena Thatha understand about the books and music? Or Christmas? How I counted the days until it arrived, waiting to lick the spoons after the cake was made, and helping Penny's sister make crêpe-paper bon-bons? How I even had a teacher say my essay on the Old

Christmas Tree was so good, I should read it aloud to the class? What would Ameena Thatha think about that?

How horrified she would be to know that I sometimes caught myself not just wishing to be at Penny's house but to *be* her. To have a mother and father who read books, listened to the radio, and knew how to dance. The only thing that stopped me from carrying that fantasy too far was knowing that, as Razik Nana would warn, it would land us all in Hell. And I was already upset that Penny's whole family and even my favorite teachers were going to end up in that terrible place. I couldn't have my whole family dragged down there, just so I could have a Christmas tree in December.

I kept my eyes on the ground.

Ameena Thatha turned to her sister. "I don't know why somebody doesn't speak to her family about the girl spending so much time in a kafir house."

"Well, you know the Parangi ways of the mother's family…"

"Still, all the things that go on in such places! I hear there's a dog there too, jumping on people and licking their face and hands."

"Aiyaah!"

"And what does she eat when she is there? They cook that other kind of meat; you know, the animal with the snout—they do."

"*Asthaufirullah*!" May Allah forgive us! "Are you saying she eats that?" Ameena Thatha's sister flapped her hands.

"No! No! But the same pots and pans, you know, food cooked in the same pots and pans."

"Aiyaah!" Ameena Thatha's sister flapped her hands again and put them up to her face.

6

If a child looks with love at his parents,
Allah writes in his favor the reward.

- Biharul Anwar, Volume 74, pg. 77

If I didn't tell my father everything about my Marshazi friends and their lives, I was selective too about what I told them about *him*.

After he left his job at Kuhaffa Hadjiar's, Wappah set up a small stall of his own at the Galle Bazaar and then went on to the wholesale manufacture of jewelry. He did part of his business in a front room of our house.

"When your father yells at his workers, we can hear him all the way down here," our neighbors at the far end of Lighthouse Street said, speaking of Wappah's exchanges with his goldsmiths and stone cutters. I believed them; I could hear him too, at the back of our large home.

At the time, the Muslims of Ceylon had a monopoly on the gem trade in the country, which was called the 'jewel box' of the Indian Ocean. The reputation was well deserved. Manuscripts from centuries ago record the abundance of precious stones found in the island and describe its pearl fisheries as the finest in the world. Ptolemy proclaimed that the best sapphires were produced in Taprobane, as the country was then called, and Marco Polo, who visited in 1293, was amazed to find rubies as big as pigeon's eggs. *I want you to understand,* he wrote, *that the island of Ceylon is, for its size, the finest island in the world, and from its streams come rubies, sapphires, topazes, amethyst and garnet.* Legend has it that from Galle had come the ivory and jewels that King Solomon gave the Queen of Sheba.

Natives taking their baths in streams and rivers picked up shiny pebbles. Miners tramping muddy pits in the mountainous center of the island dug into blue and yellow clay, loaded their baskets, and sent up gravel laden with precious gemstones of every color in the rainbow. On Sunday mornings, some of them gleamed and flashed on Wappah's glass-topped table: turquoise like the sea, red like the seeds of the pomegranate, or gold, with a band of light, like the eyes of a cat.

My father fitted the fabulous gemstones into star-shaped pendants, multicolored bracelets and necklaces of filigreed gold. Using Ceylon's sapphires of cornflower blue, the exact color of which came from no other place in the world, he fashioned peacock feather brooches with plumes fanning out in iridescent splendor.

Though Wappah sold his creations at his shop in Colombo, which he had established shortly after the success of his stall in the Galle bazaar, he supervised the work of his goldsmiths from our home at 40 Lighthouse Street. After a breakfast of hoppers, eggs, bananas and coffee, wearing a freshly laundered shirt and Palayakkat sarong, he walked into his office.

Seated on a wooden bench on the verandah, waiting for him, were the men who cut and polished the gritty stones and the craftsmen who mounted the gems on gold and silver. They shimmied a leg, fiddled with the cloths draped over their shoulders, or walked up and down the verandah, waiting for P.T. mahathaya to come out. P.T. being the initials for his father's name, Periya Thambi, Wappah wrote those letters before his own given name of Abdul Rahuman, respectfully following the tradition of writing one's father's name before one's own.

"Bathala Mouse!" Wappah would holler, to call Bartholomeus, one of his regular workers. Hiding behind a door, my brother Bunchy and I giggled as our father stumbled over the colonial monikers that were the names of his goldsmiths—it having been the fashion among the Sinhalese in the early twentieth century to bestow these on their children. But I felt a twinge of anxiety too, and hoped that no one was walking in, especially none of my English-speaking friends to whom it would then be revealed that my father's roots were in a village where people *couldn't speak even a word of English.*

"Sirrrr," the stalwart Bartholomeus would stammer, as he crept up to the glass-topped table and put down a cloth bundle. Without raising his head, Wappah untied the knot and picked up a ring, necklace, or bracelet. He turned it in his hand; held it up to the light; looked at it from afar; brought it up close. Then, he grunted approval, "Humph."

Or let loose.

"How can this necklace be fastened? Can't you see how loose the clasp is right here? Who would want this ring? If they just wiped their hands, the stone would fall out. I have to sell this to the white people; they won't buy any rubbish. It's not for nothing that they have conquered half the world."

The light from a gemstone should come, my father insisted, from deep within, to rebound on the person looking at it. The rays of a sapphire had to shine from the center, to glow like the evening star against the midnight sky. "And not," as a cringing gem-cutter was told, "resemble the eyes of a cross-eyed woman who looked in one direction and walked in another."

During quiet times, I crept into Wappah's office, leaned over the table and eyed the less expensive gemstones that lay about in open packets: yellow topaz, cinnamon-tinted garnets, zircons in orange and brown, opals with shimmering multicolored specks, amethysts, aquamarines and moonstones. I ran them like heaps of pebbles through my fingers. No matter how hot the day, they were always cold, and when I made a fist and squeezed, the stones in the hollow of my palm felt pleasurably cool.

My anxieties about my father not being a smartly dressed, English-speaking professional did not prevent me from mining his success as a jeweler for some reflected glory. I deliberately sauntered into the front verandah where his goldsmiths waited, to bask in their regard — they inclined their heads and smiled in a way that made me proud to be his daughter. The most senior of them, Danoris Samy, sometimes brought his children along and was anxious for them to play with me.

Whenever I could, I mentioned to my friends that in our house, we were careless with precious stones; and I had stories, too, to prove that. There was the time that Sheriff Nana put a gemstone up his nose and was sent to Dr. Austin on Middle Street, not in the car, but with all the speed and urgency of Ramaswamy's snail-paced rickshaw. Midway, the cart man got a better idea and pulling out a straw from the frayed seat cushion, twirled it in Sheriff Nana's nostril. With one terrific sneeze, the jewel popped out. Though it was most likely inexpensive, I never failed to tell an open-mouthed listener that *my father didn't even bother to get his precious stone back*.

But that could not be said, I continued, of the whole half-cup of jewels that Umma threw into the garden.

Early one morning, Wappah had set aside to sit in soapy water, some gritty white precious stones.

Umma, puttering around the kitchen and seeing on the counter what she thought was a cup half-filled with coffee dredge, threw the contents out of the window.

"Pick up everything on the ground that's white and shiny," our father had ordered when my brothers and I came home from school. We went out to the courtyard by the kitchen, and on our hands and knees, picked up stones half-buried in leaves and dirt.

"Thank Allah," Umma later whispered to Zubeida Marmee. "I thought all that sludge would block the pipes, that's why I threw it outside. Imagine if it had all gone down the drain!"

The gemstones were probably zircons, but if any of my friends chose to believe they were diamonds, I let them—though as a jeweler's daughter, I well knew no diamonds were ever mined in Ceylon.

❀ ❀ ❀

I was not as familiar with Wappah's activities in his shop in Colombo. But what little I did know convinced me that I had to be selective here, too, about what I revealed to other people.

The shop in the capital city of Colombo was on Lower Chatham Street, very near the Clock Tower that the British had built to instill punctuality in the natives who—so the complaint went—had no sense of time. Wappah appreciated the landmark for attracting people to a spot only yards away from his business. From where they stood on the front steps, his salesmen looked out for anyone who looked like a recently arrived white person, and invited them in to see the gem-studded jewelry that filled the showcases of P.T.H. Abdul Rahuman & Sons. In 1948, when the shop was opened, the sons were still babies and toddlers, but the name expressed the proprietor's expectation that his male children would follow him in his business.

On his letterheads, Wappah described his business:

P.T.H. Abdul Rahuman & Sons.
Manufacturing Jewelers & Gem Merchants
Wholesale & Retail
Diamond Importers.
Importers & Exporters.
Show Room: 95, Chatham St. Colombo

Though Umma and I as females spent little time at the shop, we unfailingly knew when the cruise ships that brought its best customers were due to arrive. We had an important role in preparing Wappah for the tourists who walked down the gangplank of a P&O Ocean liner that had berthed at Colombo Harbour.

This was when Wappah insisted that the trousers and coat of white satin-drill that he wore for work be in impeccable condition. Umma waited for the dhobi to bring back a freshly laundered suit. I ironed a broad tie, folded a starched shirt, forced detachable ivory buttons back into their narrow buttonholes and polished a pair of gold cufflinks before wrapping them in tissue paper. Wappah was most comfortable in a sarong, but believed he had to put on something more elegant when meeting important people. And no one was more important than these white patrons.

In Ceylon, wearing a pair of trousers was a clothing style that set you apart from "ordinary people." So unspeakably powerful was this garb of the westernized, that some individuals did not even say its name. They referred to it in code. With one finger stretched out, or two, they queried in sign language, was the man an *Eleven* or a *One*? An Eleven had each leg in in its own covering, two straight lines next to each other. A One was someone who wore a single tube of cloth, a straight line dropping from the waist. Girls too bashful to otherwise speak their preference were known to have bitten their lower lip and averted their eyes when they heard of a prospective bridegroom in sarong—they would rather not marry a One.

Wappah had been a One in his early years, and sometime after he married, decided to become an Eleven, at least when the occasion warranted. But not without asking for some changes. His tailor shaped the trouser legs to be very loose and the sleeves roomier than usual. When the finished suit was brought home, Umma made more adjustments: stitches around the cuffs to keep them from falling over, extra loops around the waist to keep the belt firmly against the middle; buttons on threads that could be made shorter or longer, and special metal studs for firm closures.

Wappah's best friend was Mohamed Abdullah Nana, a successful businessman who also had a jewelry shop in Colombo. Even on the most dignified of occasions, Mohamed Abdullah Nana dressed in what was then considered the traditional attire of Muslim men—a white shirt and coat over a crisp black and white Palayakkat sarong imported from India. A burgundy fez with a black tassel completed the outfit.

The men in Umma's family, however, wore trousers all the time, which one could expect from a family that had a weakness for Parangi ways. Her grandfather Magdon-Ismail's portrait shows him in a three-piece suit, with striped waistcoat, starched collar, silk tie, a watch-chain across the chest, and handkerchief folded into the front pocket. Her lawyer uncle, Furkan Marma, sweated through three layers of tweed while he argued his cases in the courts of our tropical island.

"Don't I know," Wappah, said, "how your mother's brother Mons who doesn't have a cent to his name, or even a proper place to live, when he goes to the police station or a shop or office, it's all 'Yes sir', and 'No sir.' All because of his full suit and that pipe he smokes."

Elevens were set apart, too, by one more awe-inspiring attribute: They could speak English.

This was a language the Muslim jewelers who had set up shop on Queen, York, and Chatham Streets in the city of Colombo, also needed to master. The foreigners who came to their shops could be young or old, wearing khaki shorts or cotton dresses, white as snow or have arms and faces deeply tanned (the ships that brought them had sailed through the blazing sunshine of the Suez Canal), from Europe or America. To the gem traders, they were all people with whom you spoke the language of the colonial power that had most recently conquered the country, and much of the rest of the world.

Wappah had never formally learned English, but eagerly picked it up wherever he could, mostly during his business dealings and in the courts, where he spent quite a bit of time making sure that no one cheated him of anything that was his due, whether it was land, gemstones or money. He pored over newspapers, repeated what he heard other people say and tried out conversations with strangers. Most dangerously of all, he sounded out with abandon words he had only encountered in print. And that, I learned when I was still very small, was not the way to do it. Not when the language was English.

I was about nine years old and eagerly turning the pages of one of Penny's books. "Look," I told her, as I came to a picture of a long, sleek boat. "Look at this yachet."

"Yachet?" Penny asked.

"Yes, look, right here." I put my finger on the picture.

Penny burst out laughing. "That's not a 'yachet!' it's a 'yawt!'"

The blood rushed to my face and I hurriedly turned the page.

I was glad no one else was around—especially no one from the Galle Fort. Else, for the rest of my life I might have been called, "Yachet Yasmin." Like "Dung-ger" Hussain Nana, whose nickname stuck to him till he died.

Hapless Hussain Nana was taking a stroll with his friends one afternoon, when they came upon a road sign propped up over an open manhole. "Look!" Hussain Nana had exclaimed, as he pointed at the big red letters written across the board. "Over there; it says dung-ger." His friends had howled and hooted. After they had stopped laughing (and according to some, wiped the tears from their eyes), they told him, "That's *dange-er*."

Those of us who did not live in homes where pater had gone to an English school and scoured Kennedy's *Latin Primer* for the rules of the third declension, did not know from the very beginning that the *h* in *heir* was silent like the *b* in *lamb*, that *heard* did not sound anything like *beard*, and that *suite* could actually rhyme with *feet*. We came from a home *where they did not speak even a word of English*.

My brothers and I, who studied at missionary schools run by Irish nuns and Italian Jesuit priests, fretted that Wappah, every time he opened his mouth, would dismantle our toe-hold on the exclusive club of the English-speaking. He mangled the pronunciation of words, absolved his verbs of any need to agree with his nouns, and plunked a grandly polysyllabic phrase anywhere into his conversation just to let people know he knew it. He had a penchant, too, for words with *bari thanam*, dignity—words he mostly picked up from his business and legal dealings, which he thought a shameful waste not to use in everyday life. When he gave a gift, he wanted to know whether the person had "acknowledged receipt." When his children did something naughty, he told them they were indulging in a "criminal offense," and if they tried to evade responsibility, he countered, "Aah, but you were aiding and abetting."

As much we could, we kept our English speaking friends and their families away from our father. But being the gregarious person he was, this wasn't easy, and we had to listen, with our mouths going dry, to his forays into linguistic territory he had no business approaching; and after he was done, exercise damage control as best as we could.

"No, no, no, Wappah! It's the lunar calendar. Can you remember that please? You should have told Dr. Perera that the Muslims follow the lunar calendar, not the *lunatic* calendar."

But we were not the only children who shuddered to think of how their fathers were interacting with people unlike us: the gem business, as we were always acutely aware, brought some of the least cosmopolitan Ceylonese, the Muslims, into contact with elite Westerners. And these merchants, steeped in tradition, were mystified by their customers, the men and women who got off cruise ships. So much of their behavior didn't make sense. Born to all the prestige of being Elevens, these were people who could have worn such dignified clothes with ease. But they didn't; they paraded around in casual short trousers and sleeveless dresses. They took a baffling interest in what was ordinary: cart men and bulls, Buddhist monks, and old beggars with beards down to their waists. They were ready to buy—of this the shopkeepers were glad—porcelain plates that had belonged to somebody's grandmother, old photographs of whom no one knew, and all manner of copper and brass items, dull and tarnished, that most people would have been glad to be rid of. The children in most families seem to have been left behind, and the husbands and wives held hands or walked arm in arm, which shocked no one since they were all infidels.

But being puzzled did not mean the Muslim jewelers lacked confidence in their ability to communicate with their customers; on the contrary, it seems they were breezily assured. If he needed to know whether the fashionable white lady seated across the table had pierced ears, Umma's jeweler Granduncle Thassim Marma would earnestly ask, "Lady, do you have a hole?"

Wappah, equally sure of himself when interacting with his customers, had no qualms about making what he thought were courteous, even required comments about their personal lives. Under bright electric lights and whirring ceiling fans, sitting across from men and women he referred to as *dorais*, milords, and *dorashanis*, miladies, he might say:

"That hat does not suit you, sir."

"Why is the lady so thin? Not eating properly?"

"Ah, madam, I have grown old, and so have you."

If told that this last could be considered an insult, he raised his eyebrows. "Don't old people get more respect?"

It intrigued me that my father could so easily be familiar with his white customers when, being the least westernized among us, he should have been—or so I thought—the most nervous. I attributed that to his character; he was not a shy person who could easily be embarrassed. But there was more to it than that. He was not invested in being socially accepted by his white customers. They were so essentially foreign that the thought did not even occur to him. It was a whole other group of people he wanted to belong to. When his children cringed to see him interacting with the English-speaking, we were projecting our own embarrassments and uncertainties to which he was oblivious. My father wouldn't have frozen, as I did, during my encounter with the pianist Peter Cooper from New Zealand, who came to Galle to conduct the examinations for the Trinity College of Music. When Aunty June and Uncle Quintus took him for a ride into the countryside, I went along. Holding myself stiff in a corner of the back seat, I didn't say a word. I no more thought of opening my mouth than if God were riding in the car.

Ruminating on the possibility of being irredeemably mortified amongst our friends, we were horrified when we heard that our father, because he could make a donation, had been asked to be the chief guest at a fundraiser for our missionary schools. Our teachers, our classmates, our friends, and any number of people who lived in the Fort, perhaps *all* the people who lived in the Fort, would be at the fundraiser. And in their presence, Wappah would not only have to take part in Spin-the-Wheel, Bean-Bag Toss and Hoopla, which foreign games were no part of his childhood, he would also have to make small talk with nuns and priests, sit down to tea with them, and—this we could barely allow ourselves to contemplate—make a speech. In English.

My brothers and I begged and pleaded that he decline.

"Tell them no. You'll cut the ribbon, but you won't make a speech."

Wappah agreed, but we weren't done. In the weeks leading up to the event, his children imagined every encounter for which he was woefully unprepared. We tormented ourselves by going over the ways in which we would be the laughingstock in the Galle Fort for months, years even. Maybe our lifetimes.

"Don't even dream of singing along when the national anthem is played."

"It's Umma who should take the bouquet of flowers."

"Don't tell Mother Superior that you are old, and so is she."

"Don't tell Father Rector that you dropped out of school and haven't even passed the second grade."

"Don't say any of that. That's not suitable conversation for a chief guest."

Then Bunchy remembered another thing.

"Wa—pp-ah," he stuttered. "If they serve you tea, you know, and it's hot—let it cool in the cup. Don't drink it from the saucer, like you do at home."

Wappah tweaked Bunchy's nose. "I won't, you impudent rascal. Do you think I don't know the ways of the white people?"

In the end, the event went off better than we could have hoped. Wappah, overawed by the presence of so many Irish nuns and Italian Jesuit priests, only opened his mouth to give one-word replies to the questions he was asked. Or so Umma reported. It wasn't something his children would have known. That day, all four of us found reasons to be as far away from the fundraising carnival as we could.

Since Wappah didn't question his certainty that he knew the "ways of the white people," his children, who were being exposed to some of the customs of these same people, didn't know how to tell him otherwise. We didn't try, even when opportunities came up, to prepare him for the changes that might be looming ahead: too wide a chasm was opening up between his world and ours.

There was, for instance, the *Time* magazine that had lain innocently on our dining table all day before Wappah saw it and pounced, outraged by what he saw on the cover: a full page spread of Botticelli's Venus, rising from the sea, without a stitch of clothing. Her long golden hair, though strategically placed, did little to hide her nakedness.

"Who brought this here?" Wappah waved the magazine in the air.

No one said anything.

"Who brought this in here?" Wappah's voice became louder.

Still, no one spoke.

"I want to know!" he thundered.

"Nobody brought it," Sheriff Nana finally mumbled.

"Then how did it get here? How can such a thing be in this house if nobody brought it in?"

"It just comes every week." Sheriff Nana mumbled again. "We have a subscription."

"What's that?"

"The postman brings the magazine to the house every week. We don't buy it."

How a magazine subscription worked was easy to clarify. What there were no words for, was to explain in ways that he would understand how a painting considered disgusting in one culture could be considered a revered piece of piece of art in another.

"No more of that! Never is such filth coming into this house again! Do you understand?"

Sheriff Nana nodded.

"There's a young girl here and I don't want her to be corrupted."

Sheriff Nana nodded again.

Wappah tore the magazine, threw it into the trash, and strode off.

Though he was confident about his ability to negotiate the alien trends that were overtaking tradition, my father didn't delude himself about the help he needed to write English. He asked other people to do that for him. Sometimes that other person was me.

I found myself penning long epistles to people I hardly knew, at ten years old. Not official letters, of course, as my father had his lawyers and accountants do that, but what needed to be written when Wappah sent money to his bankrupt cousin in Colombo, or inquired after the nephew he was educating at boarding school, or needed to communicate with his widowed niece's brother-in-law who lived in Hong Kong and was helping to support her by wiring money into Wappah's bank account.

With pen and paper in hand, he would call out, "Yasmin, come here. I want you to write a letter." Because I had been in school for more years than he had—English school no less—my father believed I knew quite a lot about writing letters.

"I have to finish my sewing. I am in the kitchen; Fathumatha is going to cook something. I have to take my bath; I have homework to do," I would reply.

"Never mind all that. Come here when I tell you to."

I would drag myself into the dining room.

He began with his standard opening lines. "Received your letter dated...and noted contents. I hope by the grace of Almighty Allah you are in good health. We are all keeping well." Then he sat back on his reclining chair, chewed the end of his cigar and cobbled together the English phrases he knew.

A few lines in, he would walk to where I was seated and look over my shoulder.

"You've written the letter without keeping a proper margin on the left side. How is the person going to file it? And what's that number? Is it a nought or a six?"

"It's a six."

"Hah! How wonderful that you know that! Listen. When you write, you are doing it to let the other person know what you mean. Your knowing it is not the point," he muttered as he went back to his chair. "What on earth are they teaching her in that English school?"

We sprinkled the epistles with his favorite lawyerly words. "With respect to the money you sent Fathima, I hereby let you know that insofar as I can, *Insha Allah*, God willing, I will give it to her on Monday and thereby she will have it before Ramazan begins." Wappah had a very soft spot for the word *Esquire* and asked that I write it after people's names; he was always visibly pleased when they returned the compliment and used it after his. He always signed off with his full name, P.T.H. Abdul Rahuman, firmly underlined and embellished with three dots below. He did this even when writing to the closest of his relatives and in the postcards he occasionally sent me, when he was on a trip somewhere.

Looking back, I realize that my stomach tightened when Wappah called me to write his letters not just because he got impatient and yelled. It was a reminder of something that I did not allow into full consciousness but was nevertheless there: that few other fathers relied on their children for such a thing. Mothers yes, but not fathers. Not in the Galle Fort anyway. I could read and write this foreign language in ways he could not; I had moved away to a culture he could not negotiate—a culture, moreover, that thought less of him for this inability. Was I in danger of thinking less of him too? If that question sometimes flickered up, it did most strongly during these letter-writing episodes.

I latched on to whatever I believed would give my father some prestige. His having a passport, for instance, was good for some standing—travel abroad at the time being a great luxury and only for the rich and urbanized. He had taken it out to make the pilgrimage to Mecca, the trip which gained him the honorific *Hadjiar*: he who has done the Haj. What I didn't tell my friends when I dropped "my father has a passport" into the conversation was that he had managed to get this impressive article without having a birth certificate, which everybody had except people in the villages. When the issuing office demanded that document, Wappah went to a Justice of the Peace in Galle town and asked for an affidavit that proved, according to his reckoning, that he had, indeed, been born. "When the JP asked when that was," Wappah recounted, "I made up the day then and there: April 14th, 1909. So that's what it says in my passport. How was the man in the government office going to know whether that was true or not?"

I chuckled right along with him so he would have no reason to think there were parts to that story I didn't want others to know.

7

*The person who severs the bond of
kinship will not enter Paradise.*

- Hadith, Bukhari and Muslim

In first grade, when Sister Bernadette asked if anyone wanted to tell how they spent the weekend, Anthony Bond, the son of Mr. Bond, the British manager of Walker's Company on Church Street, always raised his hand. (Anthony was with us because kindergarten and first grade had both boys and girls). Sister Bernadette smiled. She was happy, I think, to have the rest of us hear the language as it was spoken by someone actually from England. And we listened in awe as this golden-haired classmate told us how he played cricket and went fishing and watched his father use his hunting rifle. With his sister, Sheila, he had played Snap and Happy Families, and over a board of Snakes and Ladders cupped his hands as he threw a dice, hoping to get a six.

One Monday, Anthony reported, his whole family except for his little brother, Peter, who was too young, had played a game called Monopoly. They bought and sold houses and hotels with paper money and put people in jail when they couldn't pay the rent. Whoever became the richest person won the game.

I would soon be playing this game at Penny's, I thought excitedly. Whatever happened at Anthony Bond's home was quickly picked up in her house, though her family was not directly from England. And I did end up playing it, but not, as I would have liked, all through a weekend; there were other things I had to do.

On Saturday afternoons, I waited for Wappah to return from Colombo. The *Ruhunu Kumari* train pulled into the railway station at six thirty and for almost an hour before that, I, like other children in the Fort who had fathers who worked in the city, hung over the wall of the front verandah and looked down the road. I dangled my legs, leaned forward to see how far I could go without falling into the storm drain, and bent my head back to look at everything upside down.

"Waiting for Daddy to come?" a passerby would ask.

"Yes," I would answer, thrilled that someone thought I called Wappah "Daddy," like children from homes where they spoke English.

Ramaswamy brought Wappah home from the train station in his rickshaw, and I would first spot them at the top of Lighthouse Street, Wappah in his white suit against the black hood and frame of the cart, Ramaswamy pacing at a steady clip, his rubber slippers landing on the tarred road with a rhythmic *thwack*. Wappah's stocky figure bounced from side to side as the wheels clattered over potholes, or veered away from Milk-Albert's dairy cows who roamed the streets at all hours of the day. I stood on my toes and strained to get a better look. Wappah balanced his suitcase between his legs, and on his lap held a cardboard box tied with rope. Inside that box, I knew, would be grapes with traces of sawdust still on them, pears with speckled brown skin, and *muscat*—soft, pink fudge, dotted with cashews and dripping in ghee. Some of it was for us, some for Marmee, and, every now and then, a portion for a relative or a neighbor. Over the next few days, when I was on my way to the ramparts, it was likely that someone would call me aside and say, "That was an especially good muscat your father brought this week." I would smile shyly and walk on.

When the box was unloaded, Umma hurried to separate our portions from what was to be gifted; Wappah made sure to set aside, as he always did, his sister's share. We would take it to her on Sunday.

It was a two-mile ride in the car to Shollai, and to get there we drove through the main street of the Galle bazaar where buses, cars, stray bulls, buggy carts and cyclists crowded the road. I held my nose against the diesel fumes that belched from lorries and the reek of salted fish from the stalls on Marine Drive. Wappah swerved to avoid stray dogs and boys doubling on bicycles, and I marveled at how regularly the cart bulls plopped piles of dung on the road. Soon, the air became fresh. We passed trees and grassy fields and within minutes took a sharp turn into a narrow path of red gravel. Our tires crunched to a halt—we had arrived at my father's childhood home.

"It is never good," Wappah said, as he handed me a package, "to walk into someone's house with your hands swinging by your side. They should be holding a gift." The prophet, who had been a generous man, had said: *Exchange gifts; that will increase your love for each other*. I usually held away from my dress a brown paper bag twisted at the top and seeping clarified butter from below.

Many years before I was born, Wappah had done up his childhood home and given it to Marmee for her dowry. Mud and bamboo walls had been replaced with brick, the dirt floors with flagstone, and the thatched roof with tiles. Trees in the front had been removed too, so that you could see the house from the main road and get a good view of the roof with its clay tiles, one over the other, patterned into scallops. Glass windows enclosed the verandah, and when the afternoon sun bounced off the brass hinges it made them gleam like burnished gold, just as in some of the best houses in the Galle Fort.

Inside, Wappah had added an extra bedroom, but it remained unused. Marmee's husband,

Marma, slept on the back verandah, and Marmee slept with her children in a corner of the front room she had used as a child.

"Aah, you have come," my aunt said as she came forward to greet us. If I lingered at the doorway to scrape off cow dung from my shoe, she held me by the hand and hurried me in. "Don't worry about that; this is not *Sheemai*, you know," —London— "this is your Marmee's house."

In the early years, Wappumma was there too and we would walk straight to the back of the house where she waited for us on a wooden bed with just a straw mat spread out. She sat up as soon as she saw us and reached out to hug me, her wide smile exposing her toothless gums. I hugged her back.

My uncle, Marma, was usually out when we visited: he always had a reason, it seemed, to be away. If we arrived unexpectedly and found him there, he did not stay long. Muttering something about needing to buy beedi cigarettes from the corner shop or having to meet someone at the Kosgaha junction, he would back out of the room and be gone. Marmee did not ask him to stay, and Wappah barely gave him a glance.

Wappah had arranged Marmee's marriage as a brother was supposed to do, but it had taken some time. He had to collect the money for her dowry, and find, if he could, a bridegroom with some *shangai*—the status of belonging to a "good" family. In the end he settled for what he could get—Marmee was growing old—and married her to my uncle, with his perpetually averted eyes. It seemed not to have mattered that he did not have a proper job, or any at all. Marmee had a brother who would look after her—families searching for a bride always liked a girl who had brothers who would look after her.

Not once did anyone say anything about Marma's job—that he was going to it, coming from it or anything like that. In fact, no one said much about Marma at all, except Umma, who observed that while it was true that a brother should help his sister, Wappah went too far. He only answered: "She is my own sister, and I will always look after her." Others in the community, especially those who had relatives who helped them, held my father up as an example of what a brother should be. They reminded everyone of the prophet's saying: *He who believes in Allah and the Last Day, should maintain well the ties of the womb.*

Soon after we arrived, Wappah took a tour of the house and garden. He looked around his old home and peppered Marmee with questions. "Have those bricks fallen from the back wall? Do they need to be replaced? Are the coconuts ready to be plucked? When is the kerosene man coming? The lamps look like they are running low." He craned his neck to look at the roof. If a shaft of light was coming through, he asked, "Are the tiles broken?"

"Yes, yes," Marmee would hasten to reply. "The mongoose was running around. We haven't got around to fixing it yet."

"Someone should attend to these things," Wappah would say, the irritation rising in his voice.

"Yes, of course, of course," Marmee would answer, clasping her hands tight.

They stepped out into the back garden. If the worms were attacking the ripe mangoes or the jak fruit was yellow and bursting at the sides, Wappah had something to say about that. He noticed if the kitchen door was unhinged, or the thatched leaf fence was breaking down.

My father surveyed the neighbors' properties too from where he stood on the steps of the verandah, and usually had something to say. If it were up to him, he would not—like that idiot Sadullah Nana—build a shed where the breadfruits could fall on the roof.

When the tour was done, Marmee drew up a low stool and Wappah lay back on a reclining chair.

I should always "join in" with my cousins, Wappah said. We were kith and kin, and no stranger would help me in an hour of need like they would. I had no idea what "an hour of need" could be, but when my youngest cousin, Nabeesa, held my hand and asked, "Would you like to see your reflection in the well?" I nodded yes—even though I had seen the outline of my face in the water the week before and many weeks before that too. I joined in, too, to throw rice for the newly hatched chicken and hunt for shiny black *batta* seeds on the ground. When there was nothing more to do, we went back to the house.

My older cousins, Hidaya and Maraliya, brought out the cloth dolls that Wappumma made to where I was seated in the front hall. They fit in the palm of my hand, tubes of cotton rolled up to make faces and bodies, tamarind seeds stitched in for eyes. I folded and unfolded the legs and arms for a long while before I set them aside.

The only books in Marmee's house were copies of *Kumudum*, the Tamil film magazine that my oldest cousin Maraliya bought. I could not read Tamil, but I thumbed through the pages and looked at the pictures of women with jasmine garlands and dots on their foreheads, and men with dazzling teeth in white verti sarongs.

Maraliya, who was five years older than me, always begged to be taken to see the Tamil films that were showing in Galle. She knew all the actors, their names and ages, and the titles of the films in which they appeared. She looked a little like an actress, too. Every day, she lined her large eyes with black kohl, dipping the sharp end of a twig into thick black paste and drawing it along the pink edge of her eyelid. Her wrists she covered with multicolored glass bangles that tinkled when she moved her arms. Marmee never went to see film shows— bioscope, as it was called—it hadn't been part of her girlhood. Few elders approved of such an activity for girls, who they said should spend their time learning household tasks and praying. Sometimes though, Maraliya found a visiting aunt or an older woman in the neighborhood willing to chaperone her to a film. Then she talked about it for days, humming and swinging her hips as she walked.

When I was done with Maraliya's film magazines, had looked around the room and smiled and looked around once more, Nabeesa asked if I would like to play *Pannangkuli*. If I hesitated to say "yes," it was for no more than a few seconds. Wappah, I knew, would be very happy if he saw us sitting cross-legged on the floor, playing a game together.

Pannangkuli was a count and capture game played with cowrie shells and a wooden board with eight holes carved into either side. Players went around picking up and dropping shells, capturing everything that was in the last hole into which they dropped their last cowrie. It could take a whole afternoon of scooping and dropping before someone could win, and Nabeesa and I almost never finished before it was time to go home.

Uncle Zain Magdon said our ancestors, the Moors, had brought Pannangkuli with them when they came to Ceylon from North Africa, many hundreds of years ago. Penny, when I had described Pannangkuli, made a face. Aunty June said she had never heard of it; it was not, as far as she knew, a game that was played in England.

❖ ❖ ❖

When we talked about our weekends at Sister Bernadette's urging, we were practicing speaking in English, which, we were beginning to understand, was a very civilized language. That went along with our teachers at Sacred Heart Convent regularly warning us not to behave like *uncivilized barbarians*. No one made clear exactly what those words meant. Teachers never explained to us—girls who didn't speak English at home—the expressions they used: pay *attention*, show *respect*, be *punctual*, do your *duty*. But we figured it out. *Civilized* was mostly about being polished and having good manners, what Umma called *maruvari*, what made her tighten her mouth when I spoke over other people's voices, chewed with my mouth open, or blew spit bubbles.

Miss Solomon, our third grade teacher, cared more about being civilized than anybody else. She told us: *Use a handkerchief to wipe your noses. Use a napkin, not your sleeves, to wipe your mouths. Tell your mothers to iron your uniforms. Don't use so much oil on your hair.*

Miss Solomon had pink cheeks, curly hair, and, below her knee-length dresses, smooth white legs. With her lips and fingernails painted red, she could pass for one of the ladies in our *Everyday Classics* readers.

A few weeks after I had been in Miss Solomon's class, I asked Umma for a bottle of Cutex. She said no.

"Just one bottle, Umma?" I tugged a fold of her saree. "I want to color my nails red."

"No." Umma shook her head.

"But Penny, Christine and Amber, their mothers let them use Cutex."

"I don't want *you* to use it." Umma took up her sewing and I stopped talking.

"Color your nails with henna," Wappumma told me when I visited her in Shollai.

"Henna?" I asked.

"Yes."

Wappumma bent her head to show the copper-colored strands that crisscrossed her scalp. "You can use it on your hands too. The prophet, peace be on him, said we should use henna to be different from the kafirs. We have to do that, you know; be different. That's why our men grow beards, so they don't look like the unbelievers who have faces that are bare, like the bottoms of clay pots."

Anything the prophet did, anything at all, she said, was righteous for us to do. This is why, just as he had done, Wappumma also used a *mishwak* to clean her teeth. Snapping a tender twig from a tree, she chomped one end to soften it up, and swirled it inside her mouth, between the few teeth she had left, and all the way back to the throat. "This is good for the gums too," she proclaimed.

The henna leaves came from the garden. Cousin Maraliya plucked them from a tree in the backyard and smashed them into pulp for Wappumma, who then placed the thick paste on the top of her scalp—a cap of green mush—and walked about for half a day until the color took. With a rag she wiped the orange streaks that dripped down her cheeks. "Henna cools the head," she told anyone who came by.

Before the great festival of Ramazan, Maraliya decorated the hands of the girls in the neighborhood. They sat cross-legged on the floor while she drew wavy lines and dots all over their upturned palms. The tips of their fingers she covered in thimbles of thick green paste and the girls kept them outstretched until everything dried.

When Maraliya offered to color my hands, I shook my head. Umma wouldn't want me to use henna. Few people in the Galle Fort, and no one in our families, did that anymore, and I had been told not to pick up any habits from the villages. Though she didn't use the word, I think Umma meant it wasn't "civilized." She also said, though, that we shouldn't follow the ways of the Parangi people *unnecessarily*. But I wasn't told exactly what was necessary and what was not, and how you would know the difference.

Umma, I knew, liked their good manners and their taste in clothes; how they let one person finish speaking before the other did; how the women read books and led a quiet life, and didn't have noisy mowlood gatherings all the time in their homes.

But some other things were not so good. She didn't think they cared as much about their kith and kin as we did, else they would pay more attention to how people were related to each other. Penny shouted out, "Paula! Kit!" all over the house, without adding anything like Thatha (older sister) or Nana (older brother) to their names. My mother said that was very disrespectful. She complained, too, when some Fort Muslim families, because it had become fashionable, used the English terms *aunty* and *uncle*.

"Then how would anyone know who is your mother's younger sister and who is your mother's older sister; and how both are not your father's sisters? People should use the proper terms: Marmee, Shachi, Periumma. We should stick to our ways."

Marmee got into trouble, though, for doing exactly that.

My aunt had planned on going with us to a wedding in Colombo. *We are leaving on Friday evening*, Umma sent word. *Be ready at five o'clock.* And Marmee was ready—dressed and ready with her small cloth bag packed, quite a bit before five. But no one arrived. Not at five, or six or even seven.

She panicked. "They have forgotten me," she said as she paced up and down the house. How was she to get to Colombo now—she who hardly ever went there? And hardly went anywhere by herself? She would miss the wedding. She took off her "outside" clothes and lay on her bed.

We arrived at her doorstep the next day, on 'our' Friday evening, which was many hours later than Marmee's, whose Islamic day began at sundown on Thursday, the previous day.

"She's going to make us late," Umma fumed while she fanned herself inside the car, waiting for her sister-in-law to pack and dress again.

The driver said it was alright, we would still make it to Colombo in time.

Zubeida Marmee, Umma's cousin who went everywhere with us, explained that maybe it helped Marmee with her prayers to mark her days in the old way.

Umma tightened her lips. "Everybody, the schools, the offices, the shops, they all use the English calendar now. These people in the villages..."

Besides my mother's disapproval, I had another reason to say no to henna. When some Muslim girls came back to school after Ramazan, looking like their fingernails had been soaked in rusty water for a very long time, I could tell what the teachers thought about it. Just as I could tell what they were thinking when they stepped back from Rani Venkateswaram, the only Tamil girl in the class whose mother rubbed sesame oil into her hair. It smelled funny, and on hot days, you could tell from afar. It wasn't anything like the coconut oil we smeared on our heads. I thought we should all have used Brylcreem, which is how the stylish boys at St. Aloysius College kept their Yankee bumps in place. It had a fresh smell that would make the girls like them, or so it said on the backs of comic books.

The teachers and Miss Solomon especially, I had reason to fear, would have stepped back from Wappumma, too. The scent of tobacco snuff and dried betel juice hung around her all the time. At all hours of the day, she pinched a dab of brown powder between her thumb and forefinger, stuffed it into one nostril and then the other, and said, "Aaah!" After lunch and dinner, she chewed on betel leaves and spat out an arc of red juice, like blood, right into the drain; the stains on the walls and floors marked the spots where she had missed. At night, before she went to sleep, she sat back to smoke her hookah, the long winding pipe in her mouth, the water in the bowl gurgling and giving out the sweet scent of *abin*—which I didn't know at the time was opium—that Wappah regularly brought her from Colombo. And at Ramazan, she dabbed attar-of-roses on her wrists.

When I set about to steal perfume, I passed over the sticky attar that came in a bottle with Arabic writing and reached for the Eau de Cologne on Umma's dressing table. Its blue and silver label said *Echt Kolnich Wasser*—anything with words like that was certain to have the crisp tangy smell that filled the hallways when Miss Solomon came walking down.

I imagined Miss Solomon's house was like the homes described in our *English Readers*; homes where the bell rang for tea; where children spread white napkins on their laps and said, "Could you please pass the blackcurrant jam?"

Or at least like Penny's house, where I often spent the day.

One Saturday, while I was there, Penny said, "Mummy wants us to have lunch at the big table today."

"Why?" I asked.

"Because my grandmother is here. You saw her."

I nodded.

"But here in the courtyard, we can feed the birds." I told Penny.

"No, Mummy wants us at the table."

"Can't you tell her we'd like to eat out here?"

"No, I can't."

"But…"

Penny frowned. "What's the matter with you?"

"Nothing." I shook my head.

Albert, the manservant at Penny's, came by and waved us towards the dining room. He was usually the person I saw first when I stepped in through the front door. Always dressed in a crisp white shirt, Albert was at the sideboard in the dining room, polishing the silverware or wiping the rims of the drinking glasses. He set the plates on the table, folded white napkins into fans, and arranged the knives, forks and spoons. Albert always smiled when he saw me, and I timidly smiled back as I tiptoed in.

"Come," Albert said, walking up to me. "Lunch is ready."

"Let Penny-baby go first," I replied.

Penny skipped into the dining room. I stopped at the doorway. "Sit there, at the far end," Albert bent down and whispered. Looking straight ahead, I walked by a row of high-backed chairs. When I climbed into one and settled back against its heavy wooden rungs, my feet dangled above the floor.

For meals on special occasions, my relatives unfurled straw mats on the floor. Sitting cross-legged, we positioned ourselves, six people around each *sahan*, the shared platter we ate from. The prophet had wanted us to eat together like that—pressing close. He said it would help us be united. As we reached in, our knees touched and our fingers brushed against each other.

Umma said it was good manners to not plunge the whole hand in, and showed me how. Scooping up some rice with just the tips of her fingers, and using a delicate movement of wrist and thumb she put the grains into her mouth. When I was done eating, I had to show my upturned palm. If it was clean below the knuckles, I was rewarded with a smile. She set other rules for eating too: don't pick off all the tasty food; eat only what is in front of you; keep pace with everyone.

You lost out if you took long breaks from the food in a sahan, so with our heads held down, we ate what was in front of us, not stopping to speak very much. If a grandmother choked on a curry leaf, someone slapped her back and yelled for water. Mothers made rice-balls and dropped them into the open mouths of the littlest children.

If I gobbled down the fried chicken leg closest to me and looked longingly at one on the other side, Umma bent her head and whispered, "Don't be greedy. You have to think of other people." Aunt Asiyatha, though, if she caught my eye, said, "Aaah, she's still a little girl," and flung the delicacy over to me.

After Albert brought in the food, I turned my eyes towards Penny. When she unfolded her napkin, I spread out mine. When she picked up her fork and spoon, I curled my fingers around the metal handles and held them tight. She scooped up some rice with her spoon; I did the same.

On the other side of the table, Penny's grandmother sat upright against her chair. She had the blackest hair I had seen on anyone that old. Cut short, it fell in a fringe over her white forehead and penciled eyebrows. Her lips were deep red. From the corner of my eyes, I watched Penny's grandmother take sips of wine and dab her lips with her napkin. When Albert bent his head close to hers and asked if there was anything she wanted, for a moment, I forgot the food. Umma would have jumped if a man ever came that close to her.

Before long, Albert came around again. I had only eaten a few spoonfuls of rice. "You must eat some meat," he said, knitting his forehead. Gripping my knife and fork, I bore down on a piece of beef. Back and forth I went over the tough fibers. Nothing gave way. Albert smiled and nodded and I bore down even harder. My knife slipped and a chunk of curried meat flew across the table. The adults started and looked up. Penny giggled and I didn't raise my head till lunch was over.

Penny's grandmother, Ina Trimmer, wrote travel articles for the *Sunday Observer*. When they were read over the radio, and everyone gathered to listen around the big Grundig in the living room, we were asked to be very quiet. I didn't know many mothers who could write that much at all. I couldn't imagine a grandmother who did it well enough for the newspaper.

Mrs. Trimmer brought puzzles and books for Penny from Colombo, taught her songs and showed her how to curtsey, which she explained, was a very nice way for a girl to greet her elders. With the ends of the skirt held out, you put your left foot behind your right, and dipped. No relative of mine expected a curtsey, or knew what one was, but I could tell right away it was a very civilized thing to do and hurried to the mirror in my room to practice.

When Mrs. Trimmer visited, we were quiet and tried not to touch anything that belonged to her. Penny said she wouldn't like that.

"But you can eat what she leaves behind on her plate," I told her.

"No, I cannot," Penny frowned.

"But you can, because she's your grandmother!"

"Aiyaah!" Penny made a face.

I could have told her the prophet had said that if families ate and drank of the same food, it would bring them closer. But I never brought up his name at Penny's house. I didn't think anyone there knew much about him, or cared.

Penny called her grandmother "Aunty Ina." And the first time I heard her, I whipped around.

"Why do you call her 'aunty'?"

"That's what she wants me to do."

"But she's your grandmother!"

"So?"

"You are supposed to call your mother's mother, *grandmother*."

Penny shrugged.

Wappumma, when I was five or six years old, put down the hookah she was smoking and cupped my face in her hands. "You are my son's daughter, and I am your grandmother. Fill your lungs and say it out loud."

"Wappumma!" I yelled.

She smiled and drew me to her lap.

8

Among the dwellers of hell are
such women as are clothed yet naked.

— Hadith, Muslim

The problem with the sea, the elders said, was that it could not be screened off. It was so open, no decent woman could bathe in it. So during the days of blazing heat, when pedestal fans whirred in every living room and house maids frantically waved newspapers across their faces, when wisps of hair curled up against damp foreheads and petticoats clung to moist skin, the women of the Fort yearned, not for the cool breezes of the ocean, but for the *nalla thanni*, the good water, that brimmed from inland wells. Umma's uncle, Cassim Master, had on his estate in Dangedera a well with water so clear and fresh, people came from all over. We went there for our bathing parties.

Sometime in the morning, before the sun got too hot, a row of bullock carts lined up outside our house. We could just as well have gone by car, but rattling along in a bull-driven cart and jostling against each other when the wheels went over a pothole seemed more in keeping with the spirit of this picnic.

In a corner of the cart, our cook had stacked the lunch parcels that had been made only that morning. Wrapped in steamed banana leaves, the fragrance of the still warm rice and curry gave us some relief from the smells of old straw, dried cow dung and the cart man's unwashed clothes. We clambered in: the elderly first, the married women next, the maidens last of all. The children sat on whatever lap was available. I settled back against Aunt Zain Marmee (affectionately called by her husband's name), who never complained that I was always "reading, reading," never asked me to recite my Arabic prayers, and said nothing at all about how badly I sewed. She didn't care either that I crumpled her saree when I sat on her lap. She put her arms around me and nudged my face with her cheek.

Soon, we were ready to set off. With the swish of a stick and a prodding of the bulls between their hind legs, the cart man set us on our way. We clattered along, the bulls flicking their tails and trotting at a steady pace, dropping piles of dung on the road with a *plop, plop* that kept rhythm with the turning wheels. Cars whizzed by and bicycles overtook us. Sometimes, though, a lone cyclist weaving through the traffic kept pace with us, riding alongside, or just behind. If he went ahead, he balanced himself on one foot and waited for us to catch up. He had his eye set on a spot somewhere inside our cart, just behind the sarongs that had been hung on ropes and drawn across the front and back to screen the women, especially the maidens. If anyone paid attention, they would notice that a young female who had insisted on sitting at the far back had moved the screening cloth and was looking outside.

Someone lunged and pulled her back.

"Child, what are you doing?"

The maiden pursed her lips.

The older women shook their heads and said, "Our girls these days…"

An hour or so later, we were going up the clay path that led to Granduncle Cassim Master's bungalow where the air always smelled of fresh leaves, tree bark and newly cut grass.

It was fortunate for Umma that her uncle had a well brimming with cool water. In the sea, she would have floundered. She did not know how to swim—even though she had been born ten yards from the ocean, her grandfather's house, Jasmine Cottage, being at the very end of Church Street. If she stood on the balcony of this ancestral home and threw a stone it would clear a small expanse of tarred road and land on the ramparts that held the sea at bay. On tiptoe, she could catch a glimpse of the waves that hurled themselves against massive granite walls and burst into white foam. During the day, my mother breathed in the smell of crab shells drying in the sun. At night, the currents sweeping in and out lulled her to sleep.

Christian and Buddhist women walked the walls of the ramparts and made their way down the steps leading to the sheltered cove that was the ladies' bathing place. They hoisted their sarees above their calves, buried their toes in the sand, and let the water swirl around their ankles. When a huge wave sped ashore, they shrieked and staggered back, then held hands and giggled. "Muslim women don't do that," Umma said. I never saw her set foot in saltwater.

I can glide under water. I learned to do that much during the days when I was a little girl and free to bathe in the sea.

My brother, Bunchy, had learned to swim before he was eight or nine. While he was seated on a jetty of the Galle harbor, an older boy came from behind and threw him into the water: twelve feet deep, slimy green and awash in the onions and potatoes that fell from cargo ships. Bunchy thrashed around, sank, bobbed up and went down again. When it looked like he might drown, he was hauled out. He coughed up spit, slime and water. Someone placed a hand on his shoulder as he gulped mouthfuls of air. Then he was thrown in again. Eventually, he learned to swim.

On Saturdays, when the morning sky was just breaking into light, Bunchy and I, with our cousins Ramly and Rizama, ran out of our house, dashed across the ramparts and made our way towards Bathiri Cove. The wind blew in our faces and I yelled at everyone to stop as I brushed my thick hair from my eyes; they waited for me at the top of the jagged cement stairs. We ran down, laughing, and stopped three steps before the bottom. "One, two, three," we yelled before we leapt onto the cool, soft sand.

"You can't drown here if you tried," Bunchy always said as we piled our slippers and towels on a ledge and waded into the shallow water. The beach was a sliver of sand between the ramparts and sea. The ocean spread endlessly out, but underneath, a coral reef protected the cove and provided dozens of sheltered bathing places.

While Bunchy swam out, I took some time to look out into the turquoise sea, crunch the seashells beneath my feet and watch the waves that dumped seaweed on the rocks. Then, I took a deep breath and put my head in. My hair streaming back, I cleaved a path through water as warm as the air above. Buoyant in liquid space, I could move in any direction I wanted. I stretched my arms outwards and went back and forth. When my lungs could hold out no longer, I stood up.

Bunchy had headed out to sea to bring back coral flowers. He came back now with honeycombs of crumbly white stone. He could swim like that, holding one arm up. He was learning to be a lifeguard and you had to know how to do that to save people from drowning.

My girl cousin Rizama and I searched for colored pebbles and caught guppies in tide pools to take home in glass bottles. We chased hermit crabs and giggled as they scurried away from our shadows. Then we went back into the water, but never ventured away from where we could place our feet firmly on the ocean floor.

When the sun had climbed overhead and the skin on my fingers was ridged like the back of a seashell, I came out of the water, my body feeling suddenly heavy. Bunchy swam back one last time from the blue depths of the coral reef. We threw our towels over our shoulders and walked home, the sand clinging to our sun baked arms, seaweed sticking to our hair.

"Now that you can swim underwater," Bunchy said, "you must learn to do the crawl. Then you can go further out." I nodded as I pulled slimy green strands out of my hair. "I will—very soon."

I said that even on the last day that I was allowed to go to the sea.

Unlike Bathiri Cove, Granduncle Cassim Master's well was set so far back from the main road it made even Umma happy. We tramped through fields of wet grass to get to it. Invariably, when we were midway there, someone yelled, "Look out for leeches!" The children looked down, too late, and screamed: gobs of black flesh were curled on toes and ankles. Shinnamatha—the poor woman in the Galle Fort who came along to help the rich ladies—picked up a twig and flicked off the slimy pulps.

The well was not only set far behind, but much to everyone's satisfaction, surrounded on three sides by a tall parapet wall and screened off at the entrance with thatched coconut leaves. The women and maidens could take off their clothes without being seen. But if they had to, they could almost as modestly have changed in the open, so much practice did they have with slipping in and out of sarees in homes with shared bedrooms and overflowing relatives.

Whether at her uncle's well or in the bathroom at home, Umma wore a cloth to bathe; three yards of thin cotton draped under her arms and knotted above her chest, it fell in folds that she could easily move aside to soap her body. The religious people had said: *Allah who could see everything is more deserving than the people, so you should be modest before Him.* Holding her bathing cloth high in front, clamped between her teeth, Umma undid her blouse and dropped it. Next, she loosened the pleats of her saree. Then, in the seconds it took for six yards of fabric to fall on the floor, she released the bathing cloth from her mouth, whisked it under her arm and tied it over her chest. No one had seen much more of her than when she was fully clothed.

I had never seen a grown woman bathe in anything else until I went one morning with Penny's family to Closenberg Bay.

Closenberg was a part of the ocean deep near the Galle harbor that the Dutch had called *Kloffenburg*, "citadel on which the sea roars."

One Sunday morning, after I had slept over at Penny's, we gathered towels and pails, piled into Uncle Quintus' blue Holden, and rode past the old market of the bazaar towards the wharves where the boats were anchored. As the smell of fish scales got stronger, the road narrowed and climbed. White cliffs and coconut groves came into view; the car took a sharp turn into a graveled path and screeched to a halt. Penny and I jumped out and sank our ankles in the soft, golden sand.

The waves at Closenberg were huge, and we held hands on the shore to watch them speed up. Aunty June walked to a spot behind the car. When she came back, she no longer had on the dress she had worn that morning. Only the middle of her body was covered—in a silky red fabric that stretched across her stomach, dipped below her neckline and curved snugly over her hips. Her arms and legs were bare and against the dark, shiny cloth was endless white flesh. I stood still and stared. I had never before seen a grown woman's thighs.

When Penny tugged my arm and said, "Let's jump the waves," I made myself turn around to hold her hand. Blue arcs of water swelled and dropped as they sped towards us, and "One, two, three, heeere they come!" we yelled as we lurched over a rush of white foam. Pummeled to the ground, we spread our arms, rolled in the sand and laughed hysterically.

I didn't own a swimsuit, and for the first few times at Closenberg wore my petticoat, just as I did at Bathiri Cove. Its thick cotton skirt floated up and though I pushed it down again and again, always ballooned back. Sand collected along the seams. "Wait, wait," I told Penny while I hurried to remove the gritty clumps. She laughed and jumped a wave on her own.

On the beach, the wet cloth clung to my legs and bunched up between my thighs. Penny smoothed down her swimsuit, thrust a finger under the elastic to adjust it around the thighs and bounded over driftwood in her bare legs. I held my soggy petticoat to a side and ran as fast as I could, but I never caught up with her.

I asked Umma if I could have a swimsuit.

She said she would have to think about it, it was not something that any of our girls wore. When days went by and I didn't see her "thinking about it," I explained how much easier it made bathing in the sea, and how Penny had two swimsuits, and couldn't I just have one? She said she understood about the way the petticoat would bunch up; she would ask Wappah. He thought about it for a while and said, "Well, alright, if it makes her happy. She's still little, only nine; it's not as though she will be going to the sea after she becomes a big girl."

My swimsuit was blue with straps that tied at the back of the neck and a ruffled skirt that fell from the hips. I wore it first in my bedroom. Kicking my legs high, spreading them wide, I pranced and twirled. The elastic stayed smooth; the cloth was snug against my body.

"What is elder sister thinking, letting her wear such a thing?" my Shachi, Umma's younger sister Haleema, said to her husband when she saw it a few weeks later. "She might as well be wearing nothing at all."

I didn't bring my swimsuit with me to Granduncle Cassim Master's bungalow. Umma had said, no, she didn't want me wearing it when my cousins and aunts were around. It wasn't something anyone wore for a bath at a well; it wasn't something any óf my relatives wore for a bath of any kind.

I hurried to unbutton my dress and step out in my petticoat, but I had to wait my turn to bathe. Grandaunt Mariam Marmee was to go first. Shinnamatha led her by the hand to a cement bench, warning her all the while about the algae that circled the well. Mariam Marmee said she really should be having hot baths at her age, but how could anyone resist the water in her brother's well, the freshest and clearest for miles around? Shinnamatha nodded. "Ah, we are glad you came. This *nalla thanni*, this pure water, will do you good." Loosening the minuscule knot of hair at the back of the old lady's head, she gently poured a cup of water through the grey strands.

Soon, Shinnamatha was ready to draw water for everybody else and I stood by her side. Her arms being strong from pounding rice grains, she deftly lowered the rope and hauled up a bucket full of water. It swayed, and for a minute looked like it might tip over, but she steadied it with a firm grasp.

I took a deep breath. A cold stream came crashing on my head. My teeth chattered and my hair stood on end. Another bucket followed, then another. By the third torrent, the shock was over. I stopped hopping from foot to foot and put my tongue out to catch drops of water that were fresh and tangy and nearly sweet. Haleema Shachi came over with a smooth stone and asked me to lift my petticoat. "We need to get all the dirt out," she said as she soaped and scrubbed my skin, while I stretched out a foot and made patterns on the white foam that was snaking its way into the drain.

"You need to rub down thoroughly or you will catch cold," Zain Marmee said, as I lined up for one of the towels we shared. She rubbed the fuzzy cloth into my hair and whipped my head in every direction to catch the last wet strand. Feeling clean and fresh, I closed my eyes and leaned into her.

After our baths, we would drink the cool water of the coconuts that Sirisena, Granduncle Cassim Master's gardener, would pluck for us. Sirisena, like the cart man who brought us here, was allowed to be around the women and girls in ways no other men were. They were let in to sweep our courtyards, clear our rubbish bins or paint our bedrooms. While sweat dripped from sunburned chests and arms, and paint dust stuck to eyelashes, they squatted on the roof to repair the tiles, bent down to snake wires into clogged drains, or lifted their sinewy arms above their heads to bring down an axe on firewood.

When such men were allowed in the women's quarters, no one questioned it— it wasn't practical to keep out people who were so integral a part of the household. But there was a deeper explanation too. In this case, the unpermitted *male* was considered a common laborer; not in anyone's wildest dreams was he a man who could attract "our girls." Where marriage was inconceivable, romance must be too. Or so the elders seemed to have believed, until it was proven otherwise.

Twisting the bottom of his sarong into a thick rope, Sirisena brought it between his legs and tucked it at the back to make a loincloth that looped high above his thighs. Next, with the handle of a curved knife secured at his waist, he pressed the soles of his feet against the bottom of the coconut tree and climbed the skinny trunk to the top, his legs like a frog's, vaulting upwards. If there was a maiden who had taken note of Sirisena's muscles as they tensed with every upward thrust, she kept it to herself.

We waited eagerly for Sirisena to slide down the tree with a bunch of King coconuts. The sun being overhead, our throats were parched, and at last he handed them out. The tops lopped off and a drinking hole carved in the middle, when we tilted the cone-shaped fruit and took short sips, the sweet liquid would dribble down our necks.

When a maiden stepped forward to take a coconut directly from Sirisena, Shinnamatha

sprang ahead. "I will get that for you!" The
gardener, sitting on his haunches, poised on the
balls of his feet, kept his eyes on the ground and
said nothing.

Soon, we sat cross-legged under the shade of
a breadfruit tree and opened our rice packets. I
gobbled down fried prawns and pieces of roast
beef. Mariam Marmee chewed her food between
toothless gums. When we were done, Shinnamatha
wiped her mouth with the end of her saree,
gathered up the banana leaves and ordered us to
step back while she picked up fallen grains of rice
between her jagged finger nails. It would go to the
chickens, not end up in the garbage—rice being
what nourished us all.

As the sun warmed the grass, I lay my head on
Zain Marmee's lap and she ran her broad fingers
through my hair, untangling the knots, her hands
moving in and out. In the distance, I could see
my petticoat hung up to dry between the bathing
cloths. Soon, I fell asleep.

9

*Stay with the group, for the wolf eats the
sheep that strays away from the herd.*

– Hadith, Abu Dawood

I didn't wear my swimsuit at bathing parties
so no one would talk about me. For the same reason, I sat quietly during mowloods and moved
my lips along, pretending I knew the words to all
the holy verses. Blending in was important at all
times; even more so at prayer gatherings where
we united as a community.

Umma's uncle Zain Magdon did not care about
any of that. *Keep the mosque attached to your heart*,
the faithful were told; he gave it a wide berth.
Ever since a loudspeaker had been installed, and
the muezzin's call to prayer reached the furthest
corners of the Galle Fort, no man had any excuse
to stay away from the white-domed building with
the marble floors and four minarets. But Uncle
Zain, even when he walked right by, refused
to step in. He preferred to play bridge at the
Gymkhana Club with District Judge T. W. Roberts,

or keep up his skills as the billiard champion of the Galle YMCA. When the pious spoke to him about the wrath of God, he whipped around and demanded: "Where's the proof?" Nobody wanted to debate Uncle Zain's lawyerly mind.

His older brother, Periya Marma, shook his head. "Is it all those books he reads?"

To those who did gather in the mosque, the imam said: *Stand close, shoulder to shoulder, leave no empty spaces between you, else Satan will swoop in to fill those spots*. Five times a day, the men came together, washed their faces and hands from the same tank of water, wiped their feet on the same rug and stood straight: shoulders, arms and legs together. They bowed, bent at the waist, touched their foreheads to the ground and sat back on their heels—an unbroken line moving as though it belonged to one body.

The women prayed alone—the best mosque for them, the prophet had said, was the innermost part of their houses. But they left no room for Satan, either. They gathered in their homes for every religious commemoration they could think of: to celebrate the prophet's birthday, the piety of his daughter, the victory of the Battle of Badr, the life of a saint, or just because it had been a while since the relatives had got together and wasn't it time? Husbands said that was carrying their fight with Satan too far and grumbled, "If she has five pounds of plantains and five pounds of brinjals in the kitchen, she wants to have a *mowlood*."

Relatives and neighbors came together regularly for this communal prayer. They unfurled tufted rugs in the inner rooms for the women and children; if men participated (which they often did, though not with the same enthusiastic frequency as women), the front halls were laid out for them. From the highest shelves of the sideboard were taken down hymns that honored the saints: sometimes they were in a single heavy tome that could be read by a person well versed in Arabic, or a collection of simpler booklets handed out to everyone in the room.

As the fragrance of joss sticks floated up, the devout sat on the floor and reached for prayer books placed on sandalwood stands. They rocked back and forth, filled their lungs with air and delivered the sonorous sounds of the Arabic language. Rolling out from deep within the throat, *laa-ila-ha illal-laah*, the voices reached higher and higher, until after one last *aah*, the breath gave out. On Leyn Baan Street, Church Street, and Small Cross Street, the chanting reached the rafters, bounced off bare whitewashed walls, and spilled out onto the streets. Even the disbelievers of the Galle Fort knew when the holiest evenings of the Islamic calendar arrived.

Umma was in trouble with the community for not hosting *mowloods*. Devout in her daily compulsory prayers, she insisted such ceremonies were not required by the religion—no matter what anyone else thought. Though Umma could sometimes be remarkably and admirably indifferent to people's talking, where some things were concerned, I did not want to make it worse for her, or rather for myself, as her daughter. I dreaded some older person shaking their head and observing that I was backward in religious knowledge and that, if Alavia (my mother), like other people, had mowloods in her house and exposed her daughter to these traditions, we wouldn't have such a situation.

It was bad enough that some relatives complained that I had my "nose in a book all the time." It would be worse if they started to wonder whether all that reading would send me along the path of Zain Marma, who had so enthusiastically picked up Parangi customs and avoided the religion. Who would want me in their family then? Ever present in my mind was my great-grandmother's reluctance to send her daughters to school after they were "big." If she did, no one would want them as daughters-in-law.

Besides, moving my lips in pretense was not too high a price to pay for the platters of ghee rice and curried chicken that came with religious gatherings. The household help would carry in the platters, steaming and fragrant, and place them on the floor. The women would unveil their heads, adjust their sarees, and reach in. Between mouthfuls they would laugh and chat. Tendrils of smoke from dying joss sticks would mingle with attar-of-roses, the aroma of crushed cardamoms, and noonday sweat; you wouldn't be able to tell the smells apart any more than you could separate the voices in the crowded room.

10

There is not any Muslim who visits another in sickness, in the forenoon, but that seventy thousand angels send blessings upon him till the evening.

– Hadith, Al Tirmidhi

Islamic traditions like mowloods ensured that relatives both near and far would mill around Wappah, so he had his fill of people, just as he wished. But his luck did not extend to all areas of his life. His immediate family did not enthusiastically support, at least not to the extent he desired, his longing to have people about when he was sick.

Laid up with a fever, he believed he would recover sooner if he had the constant care of his family, frequent visits from close relatives and at least occasional inquiries from more distant connections. Umma did not agree. She held that an invalid needed periods of undisturbed rest. Her guide in all matters relating to the health of her family was a self-help manual published in the early twentieth century, in England: *Every Woman's Home Doctor*. Here, she found recipes for arrowroot pudding and barley water, and instructions on how to make a bed with sharply folded hospital corners. In it, a woman could also find the proper way to wear a corset and how to place a gas mask on the face. Among the illustrations in this heavy tome was one of the *Ideal Sick Room*. The Ideal Sick Room had thermometers, hot water bottles, rubber sheets, bedpans and extra thick blankets, but no relatives.

"In England," Fatheela Marmee said, "they like to be left alone." She was considered knowledgeable about such things on account of the years her brother Ahamed had lived abroad. "The babies are left to sleep by themselves; grandmothers are left to live by themselves; even the sick—one or two visitors. No more."

"Really?" someone asked. Umma's cousins had gathered for their usual afternoon tea and gossip.

"Yes. And you know how they find out that an old person has died?"

"How?"

"The milk bottles collect on the doorstep. The neighbors notice that nobody has been taking them in, and they call the police who break through the front door, to find the body—already rotting."

Everyone shuddered. Except Umma, who did not believe everything she was told, and, moreover, had a sneaking regard for the Parangi tradition of being left alone.

One day, when I was about eight, Wappah was so seriously laid up, people came to our house in numbers as would have satisfied even him.

Umma was saying her evening prayers and I was getting ready for bed when Sunil, our houseboy, came bursting into the house, yelling that the "master has fallen!"

"Fallen how? Where?"

"I don't know. I can see down the road. He's being carried. Come and look!"

We rushed out. A crowd of people was running towards our house. In the distance were some men carrying on their shoulders what looked like a motionless figure. While Sunil and my brothers ran down the road, Umma covered her head with the end of her saree and leaned over the verandah wall to get a better look. She couldn't go out into a group of male strangers in the middle of the road. Being still a little girl I could have done that, but Umma kept me by her side.

"A firecracker fell on his head," the first man to run up said, gasping for breath.

My father had gone to see the fireworks display that was part of a wedding celebration at Eglington House, the home of the wealthy Abdul Caders. He had taken us too, but we came back in time for bed. Wappah, as usual, wanted to stay till the very end. My mother wasn't interested. "If you've seen one, you've seen them all," she said of fireworks and other entertainment. Her husband, though, had quite another opinion.

If a religious procession of any kind was due to go by, he wanted to be informed early so that he could position himself for the best view. When it was Vesak, and scenes from the life of the Buddha decorated street corners, he took us to see them. We even wandered into the *dansal* tents where they gave out free food and drinks though it was supposed to be only for Buddhists. If no one else wanted to go to the zoo again, not his children, not even the houseboy, he went by himself. Naturally, on this day of celebration, he had his eyes fixed on the bursts of fire that lit the sky and not on what might be falling on his head.

Somebody ran to get our family physician, Dr. Austin Perera, and somebody else went to fetch Marmee from Shollai. Dr. Perera said Wappah was not in any great danger. He had had a serious concussion, but would recover in time. "Let no one disturb him," he advised. Umma nodded readily.

Gathering outside the bedroom and all over the house were the people who had accompanied the unconscious Wappah, and those who had heard about his accident, which was nearly everyone in the Galle Fort. Or so it seemed to me. They had come to pay the obligatory sickbed visit. Those who had hurried into the house ahead of the men carrying him were, technically speaking, paying a sick-bed visit even before the bed was occupied.

A buzz of voices filled the rooms. Some people asked my mother how they could help. Could they cook some food? Should they send one of their housemaids? Others talked in whispers. Among them were those who had come to determine how much the invalid deserved his injury, and whether or not there was any negligence in the care his family was giving him. *What on earth prompted him to get so carelessly close to the fireworks? You notice, he is not very religious? Does not say his daily prayers. Ridicules our holy men. Only comes to the mosque on Fridays. That Austin Perera is only an ordinary doctor; why have they not called in a specialist?*

It could be an act of impiety to counteract with too much kindness what had all the signs of being a judgment of God.

People spoke excitedly about when they first got the news, and how they told their neighbors, and hurried over in just the clothes they were wearing at home.

My mother tried to make them all talk less loudly, but to no avail. They lowered their voices for a few minutes and raised them again after she moved on.

And all the while, the housemaids poured soft drinks and handed out tea and coffee on tray after tray to those who kept coming and going out of our house.

Young as I was, I could have been expected to be consumed with anxiety for Wappah. I can't say I was not. But I also savored the experience of having so many people about. That rarely happened in our house! People who, as I walked about from room to room, were not loath to pat my head or address kind words to the poor daughter of a person who had suffered such an injury.

In time, Marmee arrived with her son. She had a dazed look on her face and with one hand held up the saree she had thrown on herself—it looked like it might come apart at any moment. Cutting a swath through the people who filled the halls, she went into the main bedroom. There, she fell over Wappah, one side of whose face was bruised purple.

Clutching his feet, she wept. "Thambi, what happened to you? What happened to you? Can you speak to me? Can you open your eyes?"

Marmee's crying brought us all back into the room. My mother tightened her mouth and watched as her sister-in-law continued to wail, stroke Wappah's arms, and press her cheek to his shoulder. "Is there nothing else to be done?" she asked. "Some fermentation with hot oil? A little water on his lips? Would that not help?" My mother abruptly replied, "The doctor said he needs quiet. Complete silence."

Although her eyes continued to well up, Marmee stopped wailing. But when it was suggested that she join those who were outside the bedroom, she refused. She would not leave her brother while he was ill. There was no need to station a manservant by his side. She would spend the night on the floor by his bed.

I wanted to stay by Wappah's side with Marmee, but Umma gripped my shoulder and ushered me out.

Sometime early the next morning, my aunt came running out of the room. "He's got up, he's got up," she said, flapping her hands and smiling. We rushed in and surrounded Wappah. Marmee sat on the floor, leaned her head against the mattress, and closed her eyes. Then she reached for the cup of coffee that had been served the evening before. It had remained untouched on the nightstand during her long vigil at her brother's bedside.

"He had to get better," she said, as she raised the cup to her lips, "before anything would go down my throat."

Wappah looked at her and gave a faint smile.

11

And abide quietly in your homes.

– The Quran, 33:33

Soon, I did not have to hide my swimsuit from my relatives. I no longer wore it. I no longer went to Bathiri Cove or Closenberg Bay, to Penny's house or the ramparts. Umma gave away my bike. I was twelve years old, and I had been "brought inside."

When Penny came by, I had to tell her: "I can't go out anymore."

"What do you mean *out*?" she asked.

"Outside the house."

"Not even to my house?"

"No." I shook my head.

I told Penny I could not walk out to the front verandah, or take a letter from the postman, or go anywhere by myself. During the day, I couldn't walk on the road, even with a chaperone.

"Will you be going to school?" Penny asked.

"Yes, but my ayah will be riding with me in the car."

"Can't you go to other places if your ayah comes with you?"

"No."

"Then why do they let you go to school?"

"Because there are only girls there."

It wasn't too long before Penny stopped coming at all.

"There's nothing to do," she said, after we spent an afternoon playing card games in my bedroom. She had found a new friend, Amber, whose police officer father had been recently transferred to Galle.

Umma let me spend half an hour of the afternoon in the front hall, behind the big windows that looked out into the verandah. She said our maid would have to be with me too, so that I would not be alone, and I had to promise not to lean out so far that the people walking on the street could see. She had another rule. She said I could stand there only if I had my veil on, properly, across my chest and over my head as it was supposed to be and not trailing on the floor or carelessly thrown across my shoulders which, she complained, is how I wore it most of the time.

From where I stood at the window, I would sometimes see Penny and Amber as they rode by on their bicycles. If they caught a glimpse of me behind the shiny brass bars, they waved.

Some months after I had been brought inside, Aunty June sat with Umma in the front hall. As she was leaving I heard Umma say, "No, it's not something I can do. I wish…no, that wouldn't be proper. Our girls have to stay inside."

In those early days, when I had nothing else to do, I went into the kitchen and sat on a low stool by the hearth, my chin propped in my hand. Fathumatha, our cook, who observed that I was spending more time in the kitchen than I ever had, told me I should watch her cook. "It will be useful later on," she said. Fathumatha spent her whole day at the back of the house, looking out on the small courtyard where we had a chicken or two, and for a short while, a peahen. She never went out into the verandah or walked to nearby shops like our Sinhalese maid, Nanda, and was glad to have another person to talk to.

"You should have had a sister, then the two of you could have done things together."

My face propped in my hand, I nodded.

Holding out a spoon from where she was cooking, she said, "Here, stir this."

I walked up to the open hearth and stirred what was inside a soot-covered clay pot.

"Do it properly, so everything gets mixed up." Fathumatha shook her head. "Your mother is a quiet person. She likes to sew and to pray. If she had a mowlood every week, like other people, the house would be full, and you wouldn't be so lonely."

Nanda said to Fathumatha, "She cries when school closes for the holidays. I never knew a child to do that."

"When girls have their own families, they have plenty to do," Fathumatha replied. "They shouldn't wait too long to get her married."

"Married? Right now?"

"No, no. I don't mean right now. In a few years."

"But she'll still be so young, she was only twelve a few months ago."

"I was married right after I became a big girl," said Fathumatha.

One day, after I had aimlessly paced up and down the inner courtyard, and turned the pages of *Reader's Digest Condensed Books* and my brother's textbooks, *World Geography* and the *History of Britain*, with a sickening feeling that I knew them all, Umma came up and put a hand on my shoulder.

"After some time, everybody gets used to being brought inside," she said. "I don't know any girl who hasn't."

Later that afternoon, I looked for my swimsuit. It lay crumpled in a corner of my dresser, and though I could tell that it would no longer fit me, I squeezed myself in. The shoulder straps could barely be tied, and the bottom stretched up, taut, from above my thighs.

Before anybody could see, I slipped out of my bedroom and got into the tank in the servant's bathroom at the very back of the house. The water came up to my neck, quiet and motionless. I stood still for a long while, and when I finally turned, my legs bumped into walls of cement. With my hands stretched out, I pounded the surface and watched the water splash on all sides. A few small ripples appeared on top and disappeared.

"I was still little and running around outside when your Marmee became a big girl," Aunt Asiyatha told me at the end of another day when I had not stepped outside the house at all. A responsible chaperone having always to be around me now, when Umma went away on trips to Colombo, Aunt Asiyatha came to stay with me.

Her being Marmee's first cousin, she was the repository of many of the stories I heard about my father's sister.

"She couldn't come out to play anymore. Or go anywhere without her mother. She stood behind the window and looked outside. My friends and I, we teased her; came right up to the front of the house and asked, 'Would you like a guava?' She would say 'yes' and put her hand out through the wooden bars, but we stepped back and said, 'come out and get it,' and of course she couldn't do that. We turned the fruit around, and wiggled our hips and told her how ripe and juicy it was, and she kept reaching, but we wouldn't give it to her. After a while, we ran away.

"During the day, when your father was at work, your grandmother, if she had to step out, would lock Marmee in the house. Close the front and back doors and tell her to stay inside—not make a single sound. What else could she do, when it was just a mother and her daughter?"

"What did *you* do, Marmee, all day, when you had to stay inside?" I asked when I visited her. Aunt Asiyatha had told me that all young girls came up with strategies, one way or the other, to "push the day away."

"I helped Umma with the cooking and cleaning."

"After that?"

"I recited the Quran."

"But what else?" I knew my aunt had not been to school and could read no books.

"I made pillow-lace."

"Pillow-lace?"

Marmee nodded.

"Every day?"

"Yes."

"Didn't you want to do something else?" I searched my aunt's face.

"Well…" She hesitated before she put an arm around me. "I was good at it; very good at making pillow-lace."

Pieces of old lace were still all over Marmee's house: tacked to the end of a chair cover, under a bottle of pink crêpe-paper flowers, or hanging from the shelf where the Quran was kept—panels of cotton netting, yellowed and stretched out. She had given away reams of it too, to relatives for trimming their blouses and underskirts.

In the afternoon when her mother had shut both front and back doors and lay down to nap, my aunt began her lacemaking. The whole village was quiet at that hour. In the midday heat, the birds fell silent, the chickens sought the shade of breadfruit trees, and cows stood motionless. Inside the little house, the trapped air hung heavy and still, and the only sound was the widow's snoring.

Marmee dragged a chair to where the lace-maker was, on a table near the window where the afternoon sun came in, and remembered to sit up straight; when it was time to get her married, her mother had told her, no one should say that her shoulders were hunched. Placing her arms on a padded wooden frame, she picked up bobbins of white thread and cast them right and left. Braiding and twisting, her hands moved fast. Every few minutes or so, she paused to tighten a pin or adjust a strand, and before long, narrow strips of lace, crisscrossed and scalloped, inched out from the other side.

As the afternoon wore on, she stretched and arched and wiped the sweat from her hands. Stopping to peer through the bars of the window, she could see the field of green grass where, not so long ago, she had run around with her friends, bare feet trampling the ground, the breeze blowing in her face. In the distance was the jam fruit tree with its low-hanging branches that even a little girl could reach. In the days when she had been free to roam outside, Marmee had stuffed her mouth with the smooth, round berries. With one bite, they split apart, releasing on her tongue sweet syrup and hundreds of tiny seeds.

Two long loops of rope with a wooden footrest hung from the sturdy limb of a breadfruit tree nearby. Boys stood on the plank, bent their knees, pushed out with their elbows and swung a semicircle in the air; around and around. "Don't do that," her mother had told Marmee, "a girl's skirt could lift in the wind." Marmee and her girlfriends had taken turns sitting on the footrest and pushing themselves up and away.

One by one, those friends had become "big" and vanished into their houses, never to play outside again, never to walk the roads during the daylight hours. Marmee didn't tell me what she felt about that and I didn't ask. She would have nothing to share but what spoke of quiet resignation. That, I was certain, was what she fell back on when it became her turn to be brought inside.

*Marriage is my tradition; who keeps away
from it is not among my people.*

– Hadith, Sunan ibn Majah

hen a Muslim married, he fulfilled half of his religion. Everyone knew that. After a girl was "brought inside," there was nothing more important for her parents than arranging a marriage.

But though the faithful welcomed the announcement of a wedding, not all nuptials were greeted with equal joy. There were the good marriages that were arranged by the families. And then there were those unions that took place because a man and a maiden (whose modesty was ever after in doubt) had expressed their desire for each other. These "love marriages" let the whole world know that a komaru had harbored lewd feelings, that her guardians had been lax in supervising her. They often turned out, mothers and aunts observed, to have more problems than the unions arranged by thoughtful elders. How a maiden had come to desire a man—the why and the wherefore of that—was left unspoken, because it was unspeakable. But after an especially worrisome event in the community, a mother walked up to her daughter, lobbed a warning— *she will regret it, you wait and see*—and hastily retreated.

"This luv, luv, luv," Wappah said, "It's all nice at the beginning. Then you get married, see her picking her nose, and everything changes."

It was a mystery to me, how he knew. The first time he saw Umma was on the day of their wedding, after her father had given formal consent and the *Kathi*, the religious official who married people, had declared them a couple.

"How would you know, Wappah?" I could have asked if that had not been a very unnecessary question.

Some days after it was announced that Umma's second cousin, Farhana Thatha, was going to be married, Kadija Marmee came into our house, wiping the sweat off her brow and asking for some cold water.

"Have you heard?" she asked, after she settled into a divan. "This marriage in your father's cousin-brother's family; it's happening because they *like* each other!"

Umma exchanged a glance with Zubeida Marmee, who was also visiting that day. "How do *you* know?"

"I know because I know. You can't keep secrets like that."

"That's not what Ismail Shacha told me," Umma said. "He thought Zubair would be a good husband for Farhana and approached that family, that's all."

"That's how they are trying to make it look; as though it was all arranged. All bunk. *She* likes him. *She* wants to marry him."

Zubeida Marmee spat out the betel juice in her mouth. "How does anyone know who a girl wants to marry? Who asks her such a shameless question?"

"That is what I am trying to tell you; nobody had to ask her; people could see that she liked him." Kadija Marmee bunched the end of her saree over her shoulder.

"They are second cousins, after all. They must have seen each other once or twice, that's all." Umma picked up her stretched cambric and jabbed a needle into the middle of the embroidery.

"Seeing? There was more than seeing. Peeping through windows! Smiling!" Kadija Marmee's chest heaved up and down. "Someone had even seen her waving!"

"We don't allow such goings on in our families," Zubeida Marmee said. "My Rahima, on the day of her engagement, saw the cake and the food and thought it was for a birthday party. That's how pure and innocent our girls are."

Kadija Marmee glowered and said nothing. Umma signaled the maid to bring out the butter cake and orange barley soda and changed the subject.

Farhana Thatha was my grandfather's cousin's daughter. Her father and my grandfather being the children of two sisters, they were parallel cousins—what we called cousin-brothers, and cousin-sisters. In Tamil, we named them *ondutta poravi*—siblings once removed. The bride-to-be was, therefore, Umma's *very* close relative.

Not for us were generic and gender neutral terms like *cousin* and *sibling*. We had a different word for the brother or sister who was older than you, and another for the one who was younger than you. A word for a true brother-in-law, *machan*, and a word for the man who was married to your sister-in-law, *shahalappadi*. Elder aunt, younger aunt, the aunt who was your mother's sister, and the aunt who was your father's sister, all had their own titles. Your nephew was your *marumahen*, your "other son," and your niece was your *marumahal*, your "other daughter." And everyone else in the community, when the relationships were not that direct, was a Marmee (aunt) or Marma (uncle), or a Nana (elder brother), or Thatha (older sister).

So what could Umma do, when her father's cousin-brother's daughter's wedding was announced, but hurry to help? A family's reputation hung in the balance when a wedding took place, and no one wanted people to *talk*: to say that the bride's dress looked like something a village girl would wear, or that the pre-wedding tables had all local food, *nothing imported*. No, what they wanted was a response such as, "Hmmm, this looks like a family with status; I wonder, that younger boy, could we make a match for our daughter?"

Umma took me along to help with the bride's clothes. Having been brought inside, it was time to have me practice the domestic arts. At twelve or so, I was good for unpicking a hem that needed to be let down or sewing plain stitches in the inside seam of an underskirt.

Fatheela Marmee, who took leadership in such matters, had made one thing clear. Farhana Thatha was not going to have clothes that were *common*, made from fabrics that looked like they had flapped in the wind all day over the textile stalls of the Galle bazaar. A bride had to have wedding clothes that people in the Fort would marvel at, and the people in the Fort did not marvel at just anything. When Farhana Thatha's entrancingly pretty cousin Rafeeka had married two years ago, The *Sunday Observer* had run an article in the society pages about her fashionable clothes—so the family had a standard to uphold. Relatives in Hong Kong would send the latest in embroidered brocades; the mother of the bride would shop at Hirdaramanis in Colombo for Manipuri silks. A little fudging would be necessary, of course. Aunts and older cousins would pull out slightly used sarees from their almirah shelves, hold them to the light and agree that the bridegroom's people would never guess they were not brand new.

Umma could be wonderfully helpful with the trousseau. When she made a saree blouse, the fabric stretched against the arms and back without a single unsightly crease, the neckline lay smoothly flat against the collarbone—the cloth looked like it was painted on the body.

"Aah, look who's come to help us. It's Yasmin." Haleema Marmee said when Umma and I walked into the sewing room. "She's the one who's going to sew the bride's dress, no?"

Someone in the room gave a small laugh.

Umma put a finger to her lips.

I went over to where Pol Kitchi, seamstress to everyone in the Galle Fort, was at a pedal sewing machine. She was guiding a delicate fabric under the needle, and as the shuttle spun out its thread, yards of silk poured out from the other side. I fixed my eyes on the treadle that went back and forth in a steady *chug, chug* as it turned the wheel. When I looked up at Umma, she shook her head. "You want to pretend you are riding your bike."

From out of her needlework box, Umma pulled out a small cushion shaped like a pumpkin and strapped it around her left wrist. She used it for holding her straight pins—refusing to clench them between her teeth and drench them in spit like everybody else. The other women gave each other sidelong looks. Alavia's nonsense, they probably thought to themselves—in keeping with the way she dabbed only eau de cologne on her wrists when she could well afford the best musk attar directly imported from the Middle-East, and the way she absolutely refused to thrust wads of money into her bodice for safekeeping. She *had* to carry a handbag everywhere she went, like Parangi nurse ladies. But there was no denying her sewing skills.

Over a yard of white silk, Umma placed a paper pattern and smoothed out the creases. "You should cut the blouse entirely parallel with the long line of the fabric," she said, while she pinned, and smoothed, and pinned again until paper and cloth held together like layers of thin pastry. Haleema Marmee and Pol Kitchi both walked over to watch. Umma's scissors glided through the fabric.

I was given a petticoat to hem and settled back in my chair. Poking the underside of the cotton cloth with my needle, and raising my arm all the way up to pull the thread, I made one stitch after another.

Eventually, the room fell silent. The Seth Thomas clock on the wall ticked away, and after several inches of hemming, I set the petticoat down and looked around. If I bent my head in different directions, I could make out the damp splotches that always appeared on the walls of the houses in the Galle Fort: a man with a huge nose but no mouth, Africa with the bottom left out, a rabbit with one ear and two legs.

On the opposite side, Ismail Shacha's cotton undershirt and a string of prayer beads hung from a wooden peg. Next to it was a photo of the Ka'ba in Mecca, a large square edifice covered in gold and black cloth, towards which people turned to pray, five times a day. That same image, usually the only one, hung in all my relatives' homes.

Umma had her back against the woven rattan of the high sewing chair. With her silver thimble poised above the needle, she made a row of identical stitches, like ants in perfect formation. My mother believed that waiting in every piece of cloth she sewed, were precise spots that would be outraged if the needle fell a pinpoint away. I was usually happy to jab in the general direction.

"Get back to your work," Umma nudged. I picked up my needle and poked it in again. The room remained quiet except for the sound of her pinking shears clicking along the edges of her seams. A pair of scissors fell on the floor and was picked up. Haleema Marmee cleared her throat. The sun streamed in from a sheet of glass between the roof tiles, and beads of sweat collected above my lips. It was getting harder to grip the needle between my moist fingers.

"Keep in line; the hem must be straight." Umma looked over my shoulder.

I positioned the needle again and pushed it in.

"No, no, that's all wrong. Rip out those last stitches and do them over."

"Umma..." I made a face.

Haleema Marmee looked at me from across the room.

"Girls must know how to sew, no?"

"Learn to sew?" Pol Kitchi looked up from her sewing machine. "Otherwise? What will they do if a button comes off from their husband's shirt?"

"They'll send it off to the tailor!" Haleema Marmee laughed and reached inside her bodice for a small glass bottle. Pouring out a dab of snuff into the middle of her palm, she pinched it up, and inhaled. When she dusted her hands and a cloud of fine brown powder floated into the air, Umma grimaced and swerved to protect her white silk.

On the day of the wedding, the bridegroom's elder sister and his three sisters-in-law, his aunts, and probably a few neighbors would examine the trousseau displayed in the bridal bedroom. They had to be reassured that Farhana Thatha had underskirts to match every color of the rainbow, that no shade had been missed; that the filigreed handles of the brush and comb set out on the dressing table was made of real silver; that the required number of silks, brocades, georgettes and chiffons, had been matched with the required number of shoes handbags, scarves, and hair slides. They would not be entirely satisfied, of course. Some sarees and shoes were sure to be dismissed as being *nothing much*. Whispers would be exchanged about clothes that did not look *that new*. Unreserved praise for other families was not the kind of foolishness a Fort person easily fell into.

One of the visitors might see an especially lovely nightdress draped over the clothes rack, and ask, "Who made this?" If that visitor had in her clan an eligible young man, rich, good-looking, and connected to the right families, women would jump to respond.

"My daughter, she took sewing classes."

"My niece Zohora, she embroidered those rosebuds."

"My little cousin Rahima, she helped with the honeycomb smocking."

It didn't matter how young Zohora or Rahima were. It was never too early to let the word out about a talent that would, when the time came, make them more desirable as brides.

Umma would have nothing to say at all.

23

*If you don't behave, I'll marry you off
to a husband from Shollai.*

— Galle Fort mother to her daughter

The desperate need for a girl to be married off was why many Fort families "ended up," as they said, with relatives from the villages. Relatives, who naturally, paid social calls.

Before I saw them or heard their voices, I could tell when visitors from Shollai had come. "Why do they drag their feet like that?" Umma asked. She said it was good manners to lift the foot completely off the floor and put it down quietly. In the villages, bare feet securely gripped rutted footpaths, but to visit the Fort, our relatives wore slippers—thin flats with two narrow straps grasped between the toes. They shuffled these slowly on our smooth cement floor.

When you entered a fine home in the Galle Fort, it mattered what you wore on your feet—or didn't. If you announced your arrival with the sharp *click,*

click of leather shoes pounding on firm ground, it meant you were a white person or worked for the government, had some money in your family or were important in some other way; you could keep your footwear on when you entered other people's houses. With slippers and sandals, the line was a little unclear. Was the wearer entitled to such trappings on their feet—a descendent of at least a moderately "respectable" family? Or was she a common person who, though her ancestors had always gone unshod, was now parading about in a pair of thin-soled slippers bought at the Galle bazaar for two rupees? Who could tell? People whose forefathers were considered *not that respectable* were expected to take their footwear off before they walked into the homes of their betters. And thankfully, for those in the Fort upset by the *pretentions of some people*, most of them did.

Those who never wore anything on their feet, ever, cart men and coolies, carpenters and lime-burners, the men who chopped firewood, the cook-woman who haggled with the fish vendor and the fish vendor himself—they trod the blazing tar of the streets with nothing on—toes fanned out and heels cracked into webs of tiny black lines. They did not expect to be a guest in any house in the Galle Fort.

Our visitors from Shollai who slowly walked in, with hesitant smiles and sometimes slippers set neatly by the front steps, were mostly people who were related to Wappah or said they were—after he had become wealthy and married into a Fort family, many more people said they were related to him. Calling on people, or "visiting" as it was referred to, was something people were expected to do regularly. People dropped by when there was a birth, death, or engagement, when a girl attained puberty or a boy was circumcised, when someone went abroad or returned from there, when a new house was built, or it had been too long and people might forget you.

"You should visit the Fort more often," Wappah often told Marmee during our visits to Shollai. He meant not just our home to which she came once in a while, but the houses of Umma's relatives, and anyone else to whom she could claim a connection.

He brought up the example of Naema Thatha, who declared that she was related to many people in the Galle Fort though no one could figure out exactly how. Naema Thatha told anyone who would listen how many invitations came her way and how many gifts she received when people returned from abroad.

"Of course they remember her," Marmee said. "She visits them all the time."

"That's what I am telling you: you should visit more too." Wappah picked up his cigar.

"But...they hardly ever come to see us, unless it is a funeral, and sometimes not even that."

"If you go there three or four times, they will come at least once."

"They don't talk to me when they see me somewhere."

Wappah waved his hand. "When we start looking for a bridegroom for eldest daughter, why would people from the Fort consider us if they don't know you?"

"I'll make some visits, if you think it might help, if they may be willing..." Marmee's voice trailed.

The visiting Shollai ladies slid their hands along the walls as they walked the hallways inside the homes of the Galle Fort. In the front halls of the grander homes, they usually found not people, but furniture. Rows of easy chairs lined up on one side of the living room, ebony divans placed near windows, massive dining tables with carved legs, and potted palms in brass urns at regular intervals on the endless smooth floors.

Should the visitors announce themselves by calling out loud? They looked around and waited. At last, a maid walked up. "I will tell the nona," she said, and after what seemed like many minutes, the lady of the house came out. "Aah, sit down, will you," she might say while patting her hair. She smoothed down the pleats of a silk saree that fell elegantly over her shoulder, after the infidel fashion. It was not like the sarees the Shollai ladies wore—the thin cottons that were bunched up over the chest and wrapped firmly around the middle.

When the visitors had made their way to a chair or divan, they sat on the edge and took off their slippers. The toes splayed, heels crisscrossed in a web of tiny lines, they placed their feet on the cool cement floor.

A long silence set in before the hostess spoke again.

"So what is the news with you?"

"It is all good news with us; how is it with you?"

"It is all good news with us too."

"Ah, yes."

At the first sign of a visit from Shollai, I announced it was time for my bath, had a lot of homework to do or was overcome by the need for an afternoon nap. After I had been brought inside, I was much more to be found at home when these visitors came, and when Umma insisted that I be polite, I dragged myself out of my room. Sitting on a corner chair during these visits from married women had become a large part of my new life.

No other relatives stroked my hair or kissed me on both cheeks so much — I was the daughter of someone whom they had known since childhood. Someone who helped them with money and in other ways. I should have been happiest in their company, but during the long silences that invariably descended, I was acutely aware that of all the people I knew, these aunts and cousins would be the most anxious to have me married as soon as possible. Not only to partake in what they hoped would be a very grand wedding, but also because they believed that an early marriage was the best marriage. In their social circles, postponing such a thing for school or anything else was unheard of; there was hardly anything more worrisome to a family than an unmarried daughter growing old. Would these relatives who had the most influence on Wappah communicate this to him? They looked me up and down, a girl of thirteen, fourteen or beyond; I kept my eyes focused on some distant spot.

Perhaps during the long silences, that were always a part of these visits in our house or elsewhere, the Shollai ladies looked through the open doorways to the bedrooms where there were four-poster beds with striped handloom coverlets. They had heard that the women of these homes followed the European fashion of wearing special long gowns for sleeping. One Fort family's daughters were even known to wear something like loose men's trousers to bed.

On the walls were framed pictures of children with golden hair playing with snow-white kittens. Sometimes, porcelain figurines were set on top of shelves. If one of these were a young girl who stood on tiptoe, wearing a short, stiff, skirt that stood straight out and showed her thighs, the visitors probably wondered about this display of a nearly naked woman in a Muslim home.

"We have been having so much rain." Someone would finally break the silence.

"Yes, so much, that's what everybody has been saying."

When the maid brought out a tray, the visitors reached for a biscuit or a slice of butter cake, broke off small pieces and popped them into their mouths. They stopped every few minutes to wipe their lips with the edges of their sarees. The cold glasses of orange barley soda that were served proclaimed that this was a house with an icebox. As the unaccustomed chill of the liquid went down their throats, the Shollai ladies scrunched their faces.

The maid exchanged a look with her mistress.

14

*And the virgin shall not be married
until her consent is obtained.*

– Hadith, Sunan ibn Majah

O messenger of Allah!
How shall her consent be obtained?
It is sufficient that she remains silent.

ince I was not able to go outside, watching
Farhana Thatha's bridal dais being made gave
me something to do. The dais was a decorated
stage on which a bride would sit for hours, still as
a statue, her eyes downcast, until the bridegroom
she might be seeing for the first time in her life
arrived. Farhana Thatha's dais was going to be an
arch of wrought iron, over a wooden platform,
bedecked from top to bottom in the plastic flowers
that a relative had sent from Hong Kong. The
wrought iron was black, the platform covered in
pink satin, the plastic flowers in every color of the

rainbow. A man threaded these artificial blossoms through the metal curves of the arch: a red rose followed by a yellow daisy and a purple violet. Along the edge of the platform, he created a border of dark green leaves. Fatheela Marmee nodded approvingly. "Like the burst of hot chilies on your tongue," she said, giving voice to a belief that was common among our people, "decorations should jolt your eyes when you look at them."

What did the bride do, I wondered, as she sat for hours, waiting for her groom to arrive? Was she asleep? Was she counting the petals in the bouquet she carried in her hands? Was she thinking of the man she was going to marry? It was hard to know. No modest girl ever spoke of her wedding before that event had come and gone. Marriage was something only the married discussed. Brides-to-be stood up to be measured for clothes, had their hair permed into tight curls and fingernails painted red without ever saying the word "wedding."

If someone teased, "Aahye, aahye! Look who's going to get married," they blushed and looked away.

Do you *want* to marry, Farhana? Who would ask such a question? What would she do otherwise? Spend the rest of her life inside her house, ears pricked for the sound of strangers approaching, ready to bolt behind a closed door? Forever begging her brother or nephew to bring her magazines from the corner store?

Married, she would have her own family, children to raise and servants to scold. She would always be a modest Muslim woman, but she had vastly more freedom than a komaru. She could come out into the front hall and greet her visitors; could walk out to the verandah and lean over the parapet wall to haggle with a fish vendor. She could cover her head with the free end of her saree and walk to her neighbor's house for a chat. Or, walk all the way to the end of the street to look in on an ailing cousin. Some husbands were generous and kind, and the marriages were good; some husbands humiliated and yelled, and the marriage was not so good. But, any marriage at all was better than being unmarried.

Girls wanted to be a bride. They wanted to drape cashmeres and chiffons over their shoulders and with the silken folds cascading off their arm, look at themselves in the long mirrors of their almirahs. They wanted to hold out their hands while an aunt clasped a ruby bracelet from a set of jewelry made especially for the wedding. When the newly married made her visits, she would sit on a chair covered in white cloth. Someone would hurry to perfume her wrist—a drop of attar of roses delicately applied with a glass wand, and someone else would feed her food from the edge of a spoon, or the tips of fingers. For three or four exquisite weeks, she was a bride.

Unmarried, she would be a *kalavi komaru*, an aged-maiden.

Mackiya Thatha was both old and unmarried. I didn't think such a thing possible for a woman in one of our families, but the aunts and cousins who kept an eye out for even the most remotely eligible of men had, in this instance, given up. Not even an elderly widower could be found for her.

"Society did her wrong," Zubeida Marmee said. "We should all have got together and got her married."

"It's not that we didn't try," Umma replied.

Mackiya Thatha had stayed in school for longer than was usual during her time. She could read and write better than most girls her age and her elders had wanted someone equally educated for her.

"She must have wanted that too," Umma said, "but of course she couldn't come out and say such a thing."

"And she didn't have much of a dowry..." Zubeida Marmee shook her head.

Daughters had to marry. Parents had to get rid of their *komaru param*, their maiden-burden, and some families had more than their fair share.

"You must have one or two girls; after all, they are the ones who will look after us in our old age; but four, five and more than that?" Fatheela Marmee shuddered. She was thinking of Umma's sister, my Shachi, who had six daughters.

"You have to take what Allah gives; what are you going to do? Send them back into their mother's wombs?" Zainarafa Thatha shrugged.

Fatheela Marmee turned to Umma. "We'll have to get together and do something for your sister—

get the girls married one by one. But we mustn't wait too long; after all," she laughed, "they say in heaven, the men are forty, and the girls sixteen!"

I was glad I was an only daughter. No one could accuse *me* of having increased my family's maiden-burden.

Still on the subject of marriage, one afternoon, Zubeida Marmee found Umma by herself and brought up all the satisfactions of getting girls settled early.

"What a relief it is, when you have finally given them away. Everything becomes easier! Remember when Saleem Nana's oldest daughter got hit by a rock on the train to Galle and her cheekbone got smashed in? The doctor at the government hospital asked if she was married, and when they said, 'yes,' he said then there was no need to fix it."

Umma kept her eyes on her hemming.

"To leave behind a daughter who is unmarried…" Zubeida Marmee shuddered.

Umma put down her sewing. "Yes, but people go to extremes. You remember Rabia Thatha's daughter, she was dying of TB, but they arranged a marriage for her anyway. Could hardly sit straight on the *arrakatul*, had to be propped up, and she died the next day. *That* was unnecessary."

"I suppose."

"And there was that Safiha who did not see her husband for 15 years; they gave her to a man who was working in Singapore."

"But, at least she *had* a husband."

"Still…some girls like to study these days…it's alright to let them stay in school for a little longer." Umma paused. "Don't you think?"

"Eighteen, nineteen, you must get them married by that time." Zubeida Marmee looked intently at Umma as she walked out of the room. "And you must begin looking even before that, or all the good ones will be taken."

Because "all the good ones had been taken," Mackiya Thatha, who was over 40 years old, wherever she went, had to stay in the secluded maiden enclosure and not with women her age. She sat by herself, clasping and unclasping her hands while the younger girls darted glances at her. Older relatives, if they happened to be around, pitched their voices a little high and asked, "So… how are you keeping, Mackiya? How is your aunt?" Before she could quite give her answer, they turned to talk to someone else.

My brother Bunchy and I visited Mackiya Thatha's house during Ramazan. She lived in Ismail Shacha's old house on Small Cross Street with the childless aunt who had adopted her after her parents died. Umma had told Bunchy and me that we had to be nice to her; not just grab the tin whistles or five-cent lozenges she handed out and run off to get better gifts at other houses.

Getting up from a chair that had a film of white dust and pieces of rattan hanging loose, Mackiya Thatha came forward to greet us. "Ah, Yasmin," she said as put her bony fingers around my wrist. "How is your Umma? Is she keeping well?"

"Yes."

"What are you studying for English?"

"*Every Day Classics,* book four." Of all the houses I was going to visit that day in the Galle Fort, this was the only one in which anybody asked me what I was doing in school. Nearly everyone else wanted to know who had sewn my festival dress.

"In my days, it was the *Royal Reader.*"

In time, Mackiya Thatha let go my hand and walked into a room at the back of the house.

The smell of stagnant water drifted in from the open drain in the courtyard; Bunchy and I shifted from foot to foot as we waited. At last we heard footsteps.

"You must study hard, alright?" Mackiya Thatha said as she handed me a balloon.

I nodded.

"Tell your Umma that I gave her my salaams."

I nodded again before we quickly walked out of the house.

"She's always asking me to do something," Mackiya Thatha's cousin, Jabir, grumbled. "Bring the newspaper from next door, save me some ghee rice from the mowlood, buy a packet of sugar from the corner shop. She even asks me to bring her books from the library. How would I know what to get her?"

Among the Marshazi women in the Galle Fort were several who were old and unmarried. The middle-aged Miss Roberts worked at the library. Miss Rodrigo gave piano lessons. And the three

Miss Carleighs, who lived in a house just two doors from ours, walked on the ramparts every afternoon—the three of them always together, and no one else.

People said that there were so many Parangi women who were old maids because they didn't care as much as we did about getting married. Other people said, no, that wasn't the reason, all women wanted to get married, but there was nobody, no aunts or cousins who would come together, look far and wide, and find a suitable groom.

"We almost always find a bridegroom," Zubeida Marmee stated when she picked up the subject of marriage again.

"When a girl is ugly, they show her pretty sister to the bridegroom's relatives. On the day of the wedding, they switch, and what can he do, after he has signed the *nikah* in front of the Imam? He's stuck with her.

"That Saheed, from the corner-house family, he married a girl who was not pretty at all—and he so fair and rich—just so *her* brother would marry *his* sister with the crippled hand. That's the kind of sacrifice a brother would make to settle a komaru in his family.

"Once, you know, someone waited at the entrance to the Galle Fort and waylaid a wedding party. They said, 'We have a better bride for you, come and marry her.' And the bridegroom did that. Maybe they offered a bigger dowry. I don't know. But in that other house, the people waited and waited, and the poor bride nearly fainted from sitting on the arrakatul, but what could anyone do, somebody had snagged her groom.

"I don't know whether that's what happened to the Janab House people's adopted daughter, Fathuma. Maybe the man who was to marry her didn't get snagged like that, maybe he just changed his mind and didn't show up. But they waited and waited too, and no one came. And here was the girl all dressed up and everything. Somebody went outside, and just by the fish market outside the Fort, they found a buggy cart man and asked him if he would marry a bride who was all ready and waiting, and he said yes, and that's how cart man Hamim became Fathuma's husband. But I don't know that they could have done that for one of our regular girls. Fathuma was adopted, you know, so anybody would have done."

"Reading and studying is alright up to a point. But if a girl doesn't get married in time and have children, who will bring her even a drop of water when she is sick?" Zubeida Marmee folded up another round of betel leaves and looked around the room. Perhaps I only imagined it, but it seemed she set her eyes especially intently on me.

Miss Nora Janz who lived in a back room of Penny's house was the unmarried old Parangi lady I knew best. After she retired from teaching at Southlands Girls School, she went from house to house in the Galle Fort to teach Muslims girls who had been taken out of school, but still wanted to learn. She was called Janz *kalavi*, old lady Janz.

Every Saturday, Aunty Nora took a rickshaw to the Galle Bazaar, and on Sundays went to All Saints Church in a flowered dress and straw hat.

Penny and I, when we were six and seven and not yet allowed to run on the ramparts by ourselves, begged her to take us to the Sun Bastion to see the ships come into the harbor. Aunty Nora held Penny's hand on one side and mine on the other and walked us there. Along the way, if we met someone going home from work at Walkers Company, she smiled and greeted them. "Good afternoon, Mr. Solomon. Good afternoon, Mr. Andre, how are you? I am taking these children to see the ships come in."

While Aunty Nora sat on a rock and gazed out into the sea, we played on the grassy slopes that gave us the best view of the harbor.

There was no land south of the Sun Bastion of the Fort. Not a continent, or country or even a tiny island. Only 5,000 miles of water all the way to the Antarctic. Galle was the last haven for ships travelling east before they crossed the Bay of Bengal, and ancient seafarers sailing across the Indian Ocean had taken refuge in its protected harbor till the winds had changed in the right direction. Over a thousand years ago, Arab dhows sailing east to China had stopped at Galle—the sailors likely became some of our ancestors.

Outside the ramparts, on the ocean, were ships, boats and catamarans—specks in the vast expanse of water before they dipped over the horizon and vanished. Inside were the homes that teemed with kith and kin: helpful uncles, concerned aunts and supportive cousins. If a child shrieked when she scraped her knee, every woman in the vicinity came running out. Ailing grandmothers were visited every day, household help was shared, and so was food.

We called this *othhumai*, connection; without it was *thannichal*, aloneness, the worst feeling for a person to have.

Aunty Nora smoothed her hair back when the wind ruffled it and looked across the harbor. Her eyes rested on its blue-green waters for what seemed like a long time. I don't know whether she was wondering who would bring her even a drop of water when she was sick.

During the late afternoon of the day of Farhana Thatha's wedding, Umma and I waited for Wappah to come from Colombo. He had barely got out of his rickshaw before he asked, "How is Thatha going to the wedding?"

When Marmee had somewhere to go that was beyond the back alleys of Shollai, which she walked with her head veiled, it wasn't easy for her. She never set foot in a public bus. Few Muslim women did—a bus was a place where strange men could sit in front of you, behind you, or, Allah forbid, next to you. A train offered the relative seclusion of a compartment, but trains only ran from city to city, and did not crisscross neighborhoods. Marmee, when she had to, hired a buggy cart, curtained in the front and back, and took along a chaperone: a relative, a child from her

family, or one borrowed from the neighborhood—
so that she was never alone with the buggy man.
When we could give her a ride in our car, we did.

"I don't know how she is going to the wedding,"
Umma said. "We haven't heard from her."

Wappah kept a close eye on the invitations that
came to him and his sister. Which was something
that flowed with abundance from the people of
the Galle Fort; so much so, that Muslims in other
parts of the island—and Muslims were never
averse to the gathering of people—thought it a bit
much.

We celebrated the hair shaving ceremony of
a seven-day-old baby, and the naming feast six
weeks later; a boy's circumcision was fêted for a
whole week, as was a girl's entry into puberty.
People threw dinner parties before they went
abroad and again when they came back. A child
had learned to recite all thirty chapters of the
Quran, a family had moved into a new house,
a woman was in the seventh month of her
pregnancy, and the invitations rained down on a
willing community.

When Marmee received an invitation card from
the Fort—and it was the people who lived there
who had begun the fashion of printing out cards—
she handed it to Wappah. Printed on white paper,
with silver patterns embossed in one corner, it had
elaborate English calligraphy that no one in the
house could make out. But that did not matter—
they had seen who delivered it, and where and
when the celebration was going to be, everybody

knew: the people in the village would have been talking about it for weeks. A cousin or nephew of the host had tapped on the open front door and wedged the card between the hinges. "Aah," he said. "We have a wedding coming in our house, everyone, please come early." He said that out of politeness. Of course, not everyone in Marmee's house would go, and they would certainly not go early, unless the hosts were the closest of relatives. The invitation, as she well knew, was really meant for one or two people from her house, who were supposed to come only just before dinner.

Galle Fort people, as could be expected, celebrated a wedding for days. They had pre-wedding afternoon luncheons, a homecoming celebration to welcome the bride to her groom's house, a string of post-wedding dinners to honor the new couple, a commemoration of the first time the bridegroom ate fish (and not the chicken and lamb that he had been plied with since his wedding day), and the first time he went for Friday prayers at the mosque. Any other "first time" that someone could think of was excuse for a gathering too. Neither Wappah nor Marmee, though they would have been thrilled to be invited to these events, felt particularly slighted if they were not. These celebrations were only for the closest of family.

But, had Marmee not been invited to the actual wedding, where she could sit down to eat with four or five hundred guests, it meant that a family in the Fort thought of her not as a relative, or even a connection, but as a nobody.

Wappah rushed a message to Shollai, and Umma and I went off to dress. I was not happy with what I was going to wear to the wedding. I was never happy with anything Umma sewed for me. "Your mother dresses you in clothes that look like dog vomit," Zainafara Marmee once told me, reinforcing not only her reputation for being forthright, but also her wholehearted embrace of a deeply held belief in the community that if your relatives did not set you right, nobody else would. I did not say anything; I could not talk back to my elders, even to defend Umma. But even more, deep inside, I glumly agreed. No one except for Parangi ladies admired the clothes I wore.

The most popular fabrics among my relatives, when I was growing up, were shot silk and shot taffeta. Woven in shimmering threads of pink, blue, green and yellow, these fabrics had a florescent glow—hence the word *shot*. Umma stiffened at the approach of "shot" anything, and never made me a dress from any material like that—she, the wife of PT Hadjiar, people observed, who could afford to dress her daughter in whatever she wanted. From shops in Colombo, like Millers and Cargills, my mother ordered dotted voiles, Guipure lace and pure cotton. "Lovely," she would murmur, as she smoothed the materials down with her palms, her face breaking into a rare smile. So, I was sent out, even on Ramazan day, in clothes of the palest colors, embroidered with dainty rosebuds and delicate appliques, bereft of the beads and sequins, gold cord and trimmings that would have made me the envy of other girls.

Wappah did not think highly of the clothes I wore either. His relatives in Shollai complained that his wife dressed his only daughter, even for special occasions, in clothes that did no justice to his *maruvari*, his standing in society. But he didn't argue with Umma; in this, she had the final word.

A dress of light blue dotted Swiss with the requisite silk shawl over me, now that I had been "brought inside," was what I was going to wear. I would be seated in the maiden enclosure, where my muted clothing amidst all the gold thread and sequins was certainly not going to make me feel like a particularly attractive maiden.

Only a year before, at a different wedding, I had run with my cousins Shifaya and Rinoza from one end of the house to another, and when nobody was looking, swiped fried cashews off the platters of rice pilaf. We had shoved our way through the crowds to stand next to the ear-splitting brass band belting "I Have a Lovely Bunch of Coconuts," "There's a Tavern in the Town" and "Green Door." At the most exciting moment, when the bridegroom arrived in his decorated car, the band had played the Mexican Samba, which the Galle Muslims had adopted as their official wedding song. Someone had thrown money and flowers into the crowd and people had scrambled to pick them up as the sky erupted in fireworks.

Shifaya and I had fought about whom the bride would smile at first. "Me," I had said, "Umma stitched her a blouse, and she'll smile at me first."

"No," Shifaya protested. "She'll smile at me first because I am her first cousin, and you are only her third cousin."

Though I could not run around anymore, being at a function like a wedding had now become one of the only chances I got to be at a social gathering. And, in addition, there was the prospect of delicious food to look forward to. We would sit around a sahan and eat rice bathed in clarified butter, beef smothered in yellow coconut sauce, curried lentils, fried brinjals and mutton curry. Wattalapam, a dessert made of eggs, treacle and coconut milk, would finish the meal. Always helpfully provided on a separate plate, would be pieces of fresh pineapple to aid digestion.

Wappah hurried to meet the servant boy who was bringing a reply from Marmee.

"She is not going," he gasped, breathless from having sped the two miles to Shollai and back on his bicycle.

"She's not? Why?" Wappah asked.

"She has not been invited."

Wappah winced and said nothing for a few moments. "Are you sure?" he finally asked. "Are you sure that's what she said?"

"Yes, she was in her house clothes. She said she was not planning on going anywhere."

Wappah turned to Umma.

"Did you hear that?"

Umma's light-skinned face became even paler. "I don't know why she wasn't invited."

"I am your father's son-in-law. Shouldn't his cousin-brother have invited *my* sister?" Wappah had begun to pace up and down the hall.

"They must have intended to...but your sister, she lives in Shollai. It must have slipped their mind..." Umma's voice trailed.

"You have been going there now to help with the wedding clothes. How could they have forgotten? She is my sister. How long have I lived in the Fort? How long have I been part of the family?" Wappah's steps quickened and he turned around to face Umma.

"I will not go to the wedding," he said, his voice tightening, "and neither will anyone else in my family."

That night, Umma and I stayed home.

15

Whoever has a daughter, and does not bury her
alive or scold her, or prefer his male children to her,
May Allah bring him into Paradise.

— Hadith, ibn Abbas

Many centuries ago in Arabia, during the time of Jahaliya, the time of ignorance before the religion of Islam was brought to the people, unwanted infant girls were buried alive in the desert. The Quran condemned the practice and the prophet promised great rewards in Heaven for fathers who treated their daughters well.

Girls, Wappah observed, never left their families. This was true. In the matrilineal traditions of the Galle Fort, when a woman married, her husband came to *her* house, to live with *her* extended family. Forever. She never left her original home.

Perhaps for this reason, or because he had grown up with only his mother and sister, Wappah had wanted a daughter from the very beginning. He had to wait. His first child was a son, so was his second, and his third. Umma came close to the age when a woman stopped having children. I arrived when he had almost given up hope.

"Your father got his first glimpse of you through the window of the front room of 68 Church St," Rameesa Marmee, the daughter of one of Wappah's half-brothers, recalled. She was also my aunt, having married one of Umma's brothers, and being doubly related, took an interest in me.

"Somebody went to his workshop on Rampart Street to give him the news. He came running, but they wouldn't let him into the room right away— everything had to be cleaned up first. So, he pulled down the half curtain in the front window and looked in. His first glimpse of you was from far away."

"See this," Rameesa Marmee said, as she pushed back her hair and exposed an earring—a floret of sea-green aquamarines framed by three gold leaves. "Do you know what it is?"

I shook my head.

"These are the earrings your father gave to his closest female relatives at your naming-ceremony party."

When he took me to his relatives' houses, Wappah held me by the hand. "This is my *kalla kutti*, my naughty little daughter," he would beam, not minding that I was dark skinned like him.

"He spoils her," our relatives said, observing that he rarely refused me anything when I was a child—or if he did, eventually came around to giving me what I asked for. How far I could rely on such willingness, now that I had become a "big girl," I was yet to find out.

In the years since I had been brought in, I devised ways in which to "push the day away," as Aunt Asiyatha called it. Sitting at the edge of the courtyard and listening to Umma and her cousins while they chatted could eradicate a few hours of the day. The *Sunday Choice* hit parade of songs program on Radio Ceylon was some reprieve. We could send in postcards with our names and song selections, and it was considered a great honor if Vernon Corea chose to announce your request on the national radio station. On Monday morning, in school, it got you some thrilling, if short-lived fame. And all that close listening demolished a whole three hours on the weekend.

But besides all this, and more fulfilling, was the solace of the written word in any shape or form I could lay my hands on. I thumbed through my brother's textbooks looking for some history or geography that might be interesting. I re-read the *Reader's Digests* that arrived at home because we had a subscription to the magazine. And I read the whole newspaper—advertisements, classified ads, obituaries, and everything else. Sometimes, when he was not playing cricket on the esplanade, or horsing around on the ramparts, Bunchy would pick up a comic or two from the Tamil man's bookshop; I devoured these in ten minutes.

During my daydreaming hours, of which I now had plenty, I yearned to visit a place on Upper Church Street that I had only seen from the outside—when I was riding in a car or during a properly chaperoned, rare evening walk. Through the metal bars of the window, I got a glimpse of what was inside, and thought I'd ask Wappah.

He had eaten a lunch of rice with beef and breadfruit curry, a dessert of curd and treacle, and after a long afternoon nap, woken to a hot cup of tea. I brought a piece of sweet, sticky dodhol and placed it nearby. He reached for it while he puffed away on his cigar, his eyes fixed somewhere in the distance. I circled his reclining chair, opening my mouth to say something and stopping. Wappah seemed barely aware of my presence. Finally, I got up close. "Wa…Wappah, do you think, that is, would it be alright, for me, with Nanda as chaperone of course, that I could go to…"

Wappah who had merely turned his head when I began speaking, sat up and put his cigar down.

"I wouldn't be long there, just in and out, hardly anyone would see…"

"Where anybody can come and go? Where there are so many men?" He leaned forward in his chair.

"I'll keep my veil on. All the time. I promise."

I had begun to wear my veil properly on my head when there were people around, though I let it trail on the ground when I was at home. Along those same lines, a quick in and out of a building full of "strange men," before anyone could notice, was permissible. So I hoped. If there was no one to see, there could be little danger to a komaru's reputation.

"I'll come out as quickly as I can," I emphasized.

Wappah got up from his chair and turned around to face me. "What on earth are you thinking?"

"It's only the—"

"No!"

Umma came to see what the commotion was about.

Wappah turned to her. "Do you know where she is asking to go? That building across Queen's House! Who among our women goes to such places? Unknown men going in and out all the time. Is she out of her mind?"

"But Wappah…"

"No. Don't ask me again!" he practically shouted before he walked out of the dining room. Wappah wanted me to observe real seclusion. I was looking for strategies for getting by with just the pretense of it.

Umma put a hand on my shoulder. "I know, the Parangi ladies go there all the time. But our girls can't go to a place like that—it's too open, we don't know who else will be there…a public library."

Wappah had taken note of my aimlessly walking around the house and spending hours looking out on the road from behind the window in the front verandah. He announced, almost out of the blue, that he would buy me a piano. Knowing nothing about such a thing, he consulted Mr. Ephraums, the blind musician in Galle, and had a tropical model Marshall and Rose upright brought to our house. It thrilled my father. He had never thought so grand an object would ever be in a house that was his, and showed it off with great pride. Though I had no talent for music, Penny and I had giggled while we played simple duets and fought over whose rendering of "Chopsticks" was better. But now, it didn't bring me much pleasure to sit alone at the instrument and plunk out "You Are My Sunshine" or anything else.

So Umma said she would try me out in cooking classes. Sewing, she had given up; my hem stiches, according to her, looked like insects of all different sizes running in all different directions.

"Good food begins with a good knife," Wappumma used to say as she stroked an iron blade over a whetstone and ran her fingers over the sharp edge. "In my day, when they came looking for a bride, they asked, 'how finely does she chop the greens?'"

In the Galle Fort, they had begun to ask, can she make icing roses? Choux pastry éclairs? Marzipan violets? A wedding cake covered in gold trelliswork?

Umma's family was proud of their own, closely guarded recipe for dodhol treacle fudge bursting with the flavor of coconut milk and crushed cardamoms. "Don't let other people in here," Fatheela Marmee said, as she stood near a boiling cauldron, fanning herself with the end of her saree and scolding the cook to stir the mixture *properly*. Someone from our family slurped up a sticky drop from the middle of her palm and said, "Needs more jaggery." During grand annual mowloods, when the food was made in communal pots, Fatheela Marmee was always able to find a relative who was willing to hide a crucial ingredient in the folds of her saree and throw it in when no one was looking. Elders hovered over steaming pots, with sarees hitched above their ankles, and told the young girls in the family, "Come and watch; you need to learn how this is made." Most of us shrugged and walked away.

Not many girls stayed around either when they made *elisha*, a dish that had sealed the reputation of the women of the Galle Fort as the best cooks in the country—something not easy to accomplish since Muslim women all over poured their creativity into an activity that didn't require leaving their inner rooms. To make elisha, you had to pound whole wheat, remove the husk, cook it for a full day, smash it down to a pulp, boil chunks of mutton, shred it with your hands, slice mountains of onions, crush handfuls of cardamoms, scrape whole coconuts, squeeze out the milk, fry it all together, simmer over a slow fire, stir all the while, and sprinkle with rose water. It mopped up the hours for women who had nowhere to go and nothing else to do.

But elisha belonged to the past. Umma signed me up, as many other forward-thinking mothers did their daughters, for the classes in western cuisine offered by the Galle branch of the Ceylon Housewives Association. I held in for some time and Wappah was not unhappy at all when I gave up. He shook his head at the food that began to appear on the dining table—food he would not have relished even if made by a better cook: vichyssoise, chicken pot pies, macaroni casseroles, fish baked in white sauce. "Where's the chili powder?" he plaintively asked. He did not care, either, that my tomato-rose—an inch-wide strip of tomato peel arranged in a spiral—was jagged at the edges, wide in some places, and torn in the middle. What he wanted to know, after one look at the 'rose' atop a bed of lettuce, was, "Where's the rest of the tomato? Are we supposed to eat the peel?"

Umma next banked her hopes on cake decorating.

For many years, everybody in the Galle Fort had ordered their cakes from the old Burgher lady, Miss Jacotin. Though it was rumored that she allowed her cats to lick the spoons, no one could resist her triple-layered butter-cream ribbon gateaux. No one cared either, that Miss Jacotin's cakes were decorated with plain borders and a few dark pink roses set over dark green leaves.

Then, Mrs. Celia Jayawardene, who had a diploma in cake decorating from some very fancy finishing school in Colombo, came to reside in the Galle Fort and dazzled everyone. For birthdays, she created royal icing fairy castles, dolls with flounced dresses, merry-go-rounds. At Christmas, women gasped over her chocolate Yule Logs with their tiny red berries nestling against perfectly serrated holly leaves. Her cakes did not quite melt in your mouth—it was rumored that she used margarine instead of butter—but they became the fashion. Soon, all the mothers wanted it known that their daughters could decorate cakes just like Mrs. J, or at least that they were taking lessons from the talented lady.

Wappah said I could go to cake decorating classes, but because they were held in the middle of the afternoon, would have to take the car. He didn't care that Mrs. J's house, being at the very end of Church Cross Street, was practically next door, no more than ten yards away. He wasn't going to let me walk on the road during the day. Our driver maneuvered the car for a full five minutes to get it out from our tight-fitting garage, so that I could ride in it for thirty seconds to the cake decorating classes.

"Girls," Mrs. J said, as she tucked the end of her saree into her waistline, "we are going to make royal icing today."

There were a half-dozen girls my age. As I looked around and took in their exquisite clothing and presence, I suspected that displayed in their homes was their equally exquisite handiwork:

crocheted doilies, embroidered table cloths, shadow-work table mats, and what had recently become very popular—seashell flowers mounted on wooden frames. The sort of thing, the elders said, a young girl with dexterous fingers made so well.

Believing likewise, in the artistry of young girls, Umma's uncle Shums Marma had asked me to fashion some drawn-thread tassels for the end of his prayer shawl. When he came to pick it up, and saw what I handed over, he put his hand on his face. Hanging from the edge of a crumpled cloth were tassels in different lengths, grey with finger smudges, the ends frayed from my repeated knotting, untying and knotting again.

Mrs. Jayawardene told the class to break three eggs, separate the whites, put them in with the icing sugar and beat it all up. She walked by the table where each of us stood behind a ceramic bowl and wooden spoon.

I hugged the bowl, gripped the top of the spoon and stirred. The powdered sugar slowly folded into the slippery egg whites and made a satisfyingly thick paste.

Then Mrs. J made another announcement: "Remember girls, this is royal icing, not butter icing. Beat it just right, but not too much, or the flowers will dry and crumble."

"How will I know when it's right?" I bent over and asked Fahima who was standing next to me.

"When the mixture gets stiff, sort of, but not too much."

"How much is too much?" I whispered.

"Well…"

"Is this enough?"

"I'm not sure…"

"Shall I stop beating now?"

Fahima shook her head with what I sensed was a tad of irritation. "It depends on how it feels to you. *You* have to decide."

"Next time you ask me for help with your arithmetic homework," I muttered to myself, "I'm going to say, *you have to do it yourself!*"

School was the place where my classmates asked *me* for assistance. Where the teachers often chose me. Even if it was just to carry some books to another room, I jumped up when they called. Outside, I drew my veil close so people would not talk, but here was a place where I could bask in approval without having to sham anything at all.

Now about fifteen, I had set my sights on studying beyond the 10th grade, which was when almost all Muslim girls at the time, left school. I wanted to go on to take the 12th grade Higher School Certificate examinations, which, if I passed, would be the gateway to a university. I couldn't ask Umma and Wappah for help with that even if they had known anything about such assessments, which they didn't. My going out of the home they would consider unthinkable. Intentionally postponing marriage and therefore jeopardizing the whole purpose of a maiden's existence, was equally inconceivable. My teachers who didn't quite see it that way were ready to help with my aspirations, and did.

I looked up from my ceramic bowl. Mrs. J was readying to give us each a cupcake. "This is the base for your dahlia," she said. "Hold your icing syringe at a 45-degree angle and make a row of petals in the center."

I held both cupcake and icing syringe.

"Lift your hand up quickly when you've piped out a petal. Don't make it too big or it will fold over; make the rows even, that's how it is in nature, isn't it?" Mrs. J smiled.

I pushed as hard as I could and placed a smidgeon of icing on the cupcake, one petal (or what was supposed to be a petal) after the other. When it was finally done, my "dahlia base" had rows of white stubs leaning against each other. They reminded me of something I couldn't recall right away. But it came to me when I got back home—a mouthful of shark's teeth.

My royal icing dahlia could well have become the topic of conversation the next time a group of Galle Fort women got together. In fact, I think it probably did. That didn't matter quite as much anymore. In school, the teachers smiled at me.

16

No one of you becomes a true believer until he likes
for his brother what he likes for himself.

– Hadith, Bukhari

In the days after Wappah's downfall, when he withdrew in rage and humiliation, I often thought of our last years in the Galle Fort when he had been at the height of his stature in the community—commanding and engaged.

Of all the things that came to mind, foremost was how he gave his money away: to his stepbrothers and their children, to the widows of his goldsmiths, and the children of those he had known long ago in his village. When his childhood friend Mohamed Abdullah Nana's jewelry shop was burgled, Wappah gave him the money to start all over again. When Ramaswamy the rickshaw man could no longer work, he came by for a regular allowance. Still standing at the west end of Middle Street in the Galle Fort are the four houses he built for his nephew and nieces. In other places, the homes he helped release from a burdensome mortgage.

Grandaunt Najima Marmee held my hand and said, "It was your father who saved our house. My mother was desperate—we couldn't pay the loan—the bank was going to take it. At the last minute, your father stepped in."

Like most Muslims, Wappah chose Ramazan for giving Zakat charity, the third pillar of Islam that required the wealthy to give away two and half percent of their wealth every year.

When it was time, Marmee came from Shollai. She knew most about the needs of the people there. Who was too sick to work? Who had had another child? Seated at our big dining table, Umma on one side, Wappah and his sister on another, they grappled back and forth, a list of names, envelopes and bundles of cash spread out. They had to be thoughtful. Someone who was forgotten would get their feelings hurt. Someone who had lately become prosperous might be insulted. And Wappah did not have an endless amount of money. But a decision was made and every few minutes, an envelope put aside with the right amount.

When he made his Ramazan visits, the children playing outside spotted him first. "PT Hadjiar is here, PT Hadjiar is here!" they would shout as they raced home. After a few words of inquiry about everyone's health, my father pressed an envelope into the hands of an adult male or an older child. The younger children hovered around; for them, he had a shiny 50-cent coin or a crisp rupee note, sometimes still warm from the bank. For Zakat money, Wappah insisted on notes that were new though Umma said she didn't see the point, money was money. "You can't imagine how excitedly we waited for your father's visit," Sumrath Thatha would tell me. "We held up the new money to our noses for a long time."

To give to those he knew was easy. The problem was how to distribute charity to the hordes of indigent strangers that descended on well-off Muslims during the holy month. Who could tell them apart? What would prevent the same person from coming around again and again? The people of the Galle Fort came up with a solution. Each wealthy family would choose a different day of the month for distributing Zakat. They would gather the poor in verandas and front halls, courtyards and dining rooms. Once that day and time were gone, there was no more giving from that particular family. Wappah chose the 27th day of the month, the holiest day of the holiest month when a virtuous act would accrue double the merit. It also happened to be the only day that he fasted.

If I were returning from school at the appointed time, I would find our house full of people. The men sat in the front halls and the women in the back, pressing close against each other on the cement floor. Some had come early and had been waiting for hours; many were exhausted from the long walks they had taken in the midday sun. Children tried to break loose from the clasp of the adults, and those who were fasting were weak from not having had any food or drink since daybreak. The air was filled with the smell of clothes that had been slept in the night before, hair that had been smoothed down with globs of coconut oil, and breath that was parched. While latecomers tried to squeeze themselves into a sliver of unoccupied floor, those who had come early sweated and waited, shifting their weight from one leg to another, massaging their cramped feet. I kept my eyes straight ahead and weaved my way through the seated crowd, very proud to be the daughter of P.T. Hadjiar, who was so generous.

At five p.m., as soon as it was announced that the distribution was underway, people sprang up to get ahead; Wappah and those helping him yelled, "Get back, get back, you will all get your money, there is no need to push."

No one paid any attention.

Some people fell, and others tried to scramble over them; children screamed, and those who had been shoved aside swore, though it was particularly incumbent on everyone to abstain from bad words on this holiest of days. Eventually, everybody got the money they had been waiting for, and our house emptied as slightly dazed men, women, and children, clutching two rupee notes, spilled out into the street.

Then the real drama began. There would come by, the men (and they were always men) who claimed they were latecomers.

Couldn't they have their money, even though they were a little late? On this holy month of Ramazan?

Wappah peered into their faces. Was this someone who was really late or someone who had just been here a few minutes ago, back for another try? He could hardly tell, but he pretended he could. To some of these 'latecomers' he gave money with a firm, "Next time, come on time or you won't get anything." With others, he exploded. "You rascal, you misbegotten fellows! Do you think you can fool me? You were here a few minutes earlier and I gave you money!"

I didn't try to figure out what made Wappah so angry when he thought he was being cheated. I was drowning in the mortification of his language and behavior with all these people around, dimly aware that hardly anything divided Wappah from his children more than our ideas of what was socially embarrassing.

The 'latecomer' would plead again. "No, Hadjiar, no, truly, I never came before, I swear on my mother's grave, I swear on the Quran, this is the first time I am here. Would I lie to someone like you?"

"Get out of here before I whip you, before I beat you to a pulp. Trying to trick me, are you?" By this time, Wappah was frothing at the mouth and stamping his feet.

"Hadjiar, please, for Allah's sake, it's Ramazan, please."

In the end, Wappah would relent.

He chose to give money twice, rather than not give it at all.

This was perhaps a way of indulging the "undeserving," which some people observed was definitely one of the "shortcomings" of Wappah's generosity. He not only helped relatives with essentials like food and rent, he took them out on pleasure jaunts too. "The first time I went to Colombo," Aunt Asiyatha said, "was with your father. I had never been in a motorcar. We saw double decker buses and tall buildings, and ate biryani from a hotel."

A favorite outing was to the fêtes of Muslim saints at the grand mosques. During these nighttime celebrations, Wappah, followed by a troupe of women and children, roamed the open areas where, in stalls lit by overpowering Petromax lanterns (you could turn night into day, the advertisements proclaimed), vendors screamed their wares. Stuffing his mouth with fried lentils and oily sweets, he bought Chinese crackers for the boys and glass bangles for the girls.

When someone asked him about these *needless* expenses, his answer was always the same: "You have never been poor."

And sometimes he didn't explain at all.

There was the day when a little girl from one of the tenements nearby came to our house asking for ice. Perhaps she wanted the fun of feeling the chilled cube in her hands. Or she had found a half-filled bottle of soda and wanted to "extend" it for her brothers and sisters. She held out two thin hands, a girl of about eight years old, in bare feet and a tattered dress, one side of which had slipped off her shoulder.

This child's mother, like other women who lived in the tenements, came by once a week to get the money that Muslim families doled out on the holy day of Friday. What was she doing here today?

"Ice?" One of Umma's relatives, who happened to be visiting and was seated on the verandah, asked. "Why do you want ice?"

"I'd just like some, sir." The little girl smiled.

"There's no ice to be given away, and don't come here except on Fridays."

"Can't I have just a little? My brothers and sisters would like it so much." She held out a tin can.

Other people spoke up. "If you are going to ask for something, it should be something you really need, like food."

"Sir...please."

"Didn't I tell you to go away?" Salim Marma's voice got louder.

Wappah who had been inside came out. "What's going on?"

The little girl stepped forward and smiled. "Periya Dorai!" Big Sir!

"What do you want?" Wappah looked at her.

"Some ice, Periya Dorai, just a little to take home." She held out the tin can again.

Wappah summoned the maid. "Put some ice into this and bring it back."

Voices burst out from the verandah. "Now, every child from the tenement is going to be here, asking for ice. There will be no end to it."

Wappah kept his eyes on the little girl, and when the ice was brought, handed it over. "Run home with this," he said, "or it will melt."

"But ..." the voices from the verandah sputtered again.

Wappah turned around, and with a look that said he wasn't at this time inclined to speak to anybody, went back to his chair.

Besides his generosity, Wappah was known for his skill as a jeweler. Which was why his good friend Lighthouse-Jiffry, who got his nickname from being so tall—handed over for appraisal, a valuable ruby.

Before it could be returned, it went missing.

Umma said to look around first, it may not be lost; it may just have fallen on the floor.

"Are you out of your mind?" Wappah yelled. "Am I an idiot to drop a gemstone worth thousands of rupees on the floor and not know it?"

"Let's look anyway," Umma got my brothers out of bed. "Look on the floor, in all the corners, it should be round and red and shiny, you children have better eyesight than us."

The children crawled on their hands and feet.

"We can't see anything," they said.

"Of course you can't see anything," Wappah hollered. "I don't drop gemstones."

"Are you sure?" Umma asked. "You had quite a few stones in your hand when you came out of the front room this morning."

"I did not drop..." Wappah paused. "Well, I suppose. Well, alright, not that it has ever happened before, but it could have slipped out of my hand."

That morning, Wappah had stood on the inner courtyard, his back to the hallway, face turned upwards towards the morning light, eyes intently set on the jewel that he held between his fingers. A while ago, he had brought out some gemstones cupped in his hand, including what belonged to Lighthouse-Jiffry Nana, and placed them on a table. If the ruby had fallen and rolled away, it would have shone in all its scarlet splendor on our grey flagstone floor. Whoever came by could have seen it as easily as a drop of blood on a white cloth.

Wappah lit his cigar and walked up and down the length of the house, flicking ashes on the floor and going every now and then to the garden to spit.

Who could it be? The maid, the cook or the houseboy? After all these years, when no other precious stone had gone missing like that? The paperboy who came early in the morning? But he never came inside, just slid the newspaper across the floor. Who could have picked up the fallen ruby while Wappah had his back to it?

Wappah and Umma looked at each other.

Every morning, Abdul Kareem, a little boy of about nine or ten, walked unannounced into the kitchen to deliver freshly cooked hoppers. Shinnamatha, his mother, (the same Shinnamatha who helped the Fort ladies draw water for their well-side baths) made them for a living, soaking raw rice in water and pounding it down in a mortar. The wooden pestle she threw into the air, landing over and over on the grains that lay deep inside the hollow stone and crushing them into flour. Before dawn the next day, she poured out a batter of rice flour and coconut milk into a sizzling pan and made the hoppers that Galle Fort families insisted should be delivered to them, warm and crisp, in time for breakfast.

Abdul Kareem walked the streets of the Fort with a basket balanced on his head, bare feet tramping the narrow roads. The cloth he wore on his gaunt little body was secured at his waist with a knot. Perhaps it was part of an adult sarong his mother had cut into two so that he could have one to wear while the other was in the wash.

"What will you do?" Umma asked. "We can't accuse people without being certain. Shinnamatha has been among us all these years, and the fatherless little boy…"

"I know," Wappah said, chewing on the stump of his cigar. "I'll think of something. But I don't have much time. I have to get the ruby back before something happens to it."

The next day the news spread in the Fort— and it was never difficult to spread news in the Galle Fort—that Wappah was organizing a hexing ceremony to catch the thief who had stolen the star ruby. If it was not returned, that person would be cursed, would never prosper, would fall sick, and might even die.

Conversations buzzed. Who was it, who could have stolen P.T. Hadjiar's gemstone?

We lived then at 41 Lighthouse Street, which had a second floor. The upstairs was cleared and swept; the ceremony was to take place at night—hexing being more successful, so it was believed, when done in the dark. I stood behind Umma and clutched her saree as exorcists and magicians dressed in orange and red robes and fearsome demon headgear climbed up the stairs. They drummed tom-toms and chanted verses, beginning slowly and softly, then getting louder, till by the middle of the night they could be heard everywhere in the neighborhood. No one could understand what they were saying, which made it more likely that it was something with terrible power. I drifted off to sleep in my bedroom downstairs before the ceremony was over.

The next day, the star ruby appeared on the three-legged stool by the courtyard, after Abdul Kareem had delivered our morning breakfast.

"Would something have happened to him, Wappah, would he have died, if the ruby hadn't come back?" I asked, some years later, when I wanted an explanation for my memories of tom-toms beating and fearsome men going up the stairs. "Does hexing work?"

Wappah put his cigar down. "I don't believe such nonsense, child. You know what I think about the stuff they sell under the 'liar's tree,' and the holy men who trick people. But he was a little boy, you know, helping his mother. I just had to get the ruby back. I didn't want people to talk about him."

My father was able to get what he wanted by seeing what others might often miss. That's how I thought of him in those days.

There was the day, for instance, the 26th of September, 1959, when the Prime Minister of Ceylon, S.W.R.D. Bandaranaike was shot dead. A few days later, his body lay in state at the Parliament building in Colombo, a stone's throw away from Wappah's shop on Chatham Street. Unlike most Muslims, who were conservative and supported the right-wing United National Party, Wappah greatly admired the left-leaning Prime Minister and wanted to pay his respects.

"But," he said, while recounting the event some years later, "the queue was too long—winding around Beira Lake—how long is that? A mile and a half? I couldn't be away from the shop for so long."

"So you didn't get to see the body?" I asked.

"I did. I did. That's why I am telling you this story." Wappah drained his cup of coffee and put it down. "I want you to learn something. In any situation, look around carefully. You might find a solution."

I nodded.

"So what did I do? I walked back to Chatham Street and went over to Mohamed Abdullah's shop. Told him I wanted him to come with me to view the prime minister's body.

"He told me he didn't want to. I told him this was the problem with our people. Some big shot tells us S.W.R.D. is not good, that all Muslims should support the UNP, and everybody goes along with that. What did the UNP do for poor people? Nothing! They are a rich people's party. S.W.R.D., he did a lot for the poor man. I told Abdullah he had to come with me and he said, alright."

This, I could believe. Though Abdullah Nana was himself the owner of a prosperous jewelry store, when Wappah beckoned, he came. They had known each other since childhood, though they were not related, and my father took the lead when they were together.

"So Abdullah and I, we walked back to my shop."

"To the shop? Not to parliament building?"

"Listen quietly and let me tell you the story. We went to the shop and formed the Muslim Jewelers' *Sangham*." Wappah used the Tamil word for association.

"What? Why did you do that?"

"Just listen!"

Wappah continued. "The big man of the Sangham—what's the word for him?"

"The president."

"That's right. I became the president."

"You did?"

"Yes, and Abdullah became the writing person—who's that?"

"The secretary."

"That's the one."

"Can you do that?" I asked. "Form an association just like that?"

"Why not? We are jewelers and we are Muslims. Who was going to stop us?"

"Nobody, I suppose."

"Then let me finish the story. So after that... wait, wait, I forgot to tell you. Before all this, I gave ten rupees to the shop boy and asked him to bring a wreath from the flower shop."

"A wreath?"

"Yes, a wreath. And when he brought it, I told my bookkeeper to write the name of the Sangham and our names on the card. Also that word— what's that big English word they use at funerals?"

"Condolences?"

"That's the one. After all the writing was done, I told Abdullah to carry one end of the wreath, I carried the other, and we walked down Chatham Street to the parliament building."

"You must have looked strange, Wappah. People must have wondered why you didn't get the shop boy to take the wreath over."

"What do I care about all that? When you have to do something, you do it. Anyway, we turned onto York Street and as soon as we got near the parliament, one of the guards came running and said, 'Sir, sir, come this way.' He took us right away into the main hall, through the front entrance, not the back where people had queued up. We put the wreath down and they let us stay for as long as we wanted. I had a good look at the body too. One of the other guards said, 'it's good to see at least *some* Muslims support S.W.R.D.'"

Wappah leaned back and chuckled. "Now you know what I saw the first time—right?"

I smiled. "People who were carrying wreaths were being taken in right away."

Basking in the satisfaction of finding my father so clever, I didn't think about it at the time, but later, I had to ask: he often saw what other people missed. But was missing what everybody else so plainly perceived, also a part of who he was?

17

It is only when the women in the family keep their heads down that the men can hold their heads up.

– A saying in the community

Wappah's conversations with Marmee during our visits to Shollai, where they mostly talked about who in the village had arranged a good marriage for a daughter, or lost all their money in a failed business, took a different turn one day. Instead of settling back on his recliner and waiting for Marmee to begin, Wappah set down his cigar. "That groom from the Galle Fort Ismail family, the one who has just got engaged, I was thinking of his younger brother for eldest daughter."

"Really?" Marmee asked. "That family? Would they consider us?"

"Well, eldest daughter is fair; and besides..." Wappah turned to look at Maraliya who was seated by the window in the front hall. She was making hand signals to someone walking by the house. "Who is she waving to?"

"Just the neighbor's children," Marmee replied hastily. "Here, have more dodhol," she pushed a little plate in his direction. "Do you really think we will have a chance with the Ismail family? What does the boy do?"

"Works in his uncle's shop. A *thothu*, a dullard, people say. Not like the older son. That's why we might have a chance."

"Still, from a *shangakara* family like that."

"They will agree because of the dowry I will give. They have to marry him into a family that will help—how else will he manage?"

"But…"

"You don't visit the Fort often enough. You must come and mingle."

"Yes…" Marmee's voice dropped.

I looked up from the Pannangkuli game I was pretending to enjoy. It had been some years since I had been "brought in," and during our Sunday visits, I stayed, for most of the time, within the four walls of my aunt's house in Shollai, just as I did the four walls of our house in the Fort. Maraliya, being a komaru, was similarly confined. And just like me, she used the front window for whatever look she could get of the world outside.

Standing up, Maraliya moved away from the window and walked up to the hallway mirror. Bringing her braid of long black hair over her chest, she laughed when she caught my eye.

Sometimes, when we visited, Maraliya was not in the house and Marmee looked around nervously when Wappah asked where she was.

"Oh, she must be somewhere. Here, sit down, I'll make you a cup of coffee. I'll be back soon."

Marmee went to the backyard and dragged Maraliya back from outside the cadjan fence where she chatted with girls from the neighborhood; sometimes she dragged her back from inside a neighbor's house.

"What will I do with you," my aunt would say, adjusting Maraliya's veil, which trailed on the ground. "What will people say about your walking out of the house alone? Why can't you stay in the house?"

"It's only to the house at the back," Maraliya made a face.

"By yourself? Should you ever do that?"

"I have nothing else to do."

"Nothing to do? What about the work in the house?"

"All the work is done—and am I the only one who is supposed to work?" Maraliya glared at her younger sisters.

Marmee took a deep breath. "Say your prayers—finish the lace on the chair cover. A girl can always find something to do in the house."

"I can't do that all the time."

"Whether you can or cannot is not the question. How many times have I told you that a komaru can't go out like that? Your uncle thinks you're just childish. If he ever finds out you are going to houses in the neighborhood, that'll be the end of me."

"I wanted to be with the back-house girls—we were listening to the radio, that's all."

"That's all? *Subhanallah*! What are you talking about? Their brothers, their father, they all go in and out of the house. Bare-bodied, after their baths. Can *you* be there as well?"

Maraliya swept her long hair into a knot and strode into the house.

People had begun to talk about Maraliya's gallivanting. Haseena Marmee observed to Umma that an early marriage would be the best thing and Wappah was the person who would arrange that, but who was going to talk to him? Who was going to tell him that about his niece—his own sister's daughter, his *marumahal*, his other daughter? Wappah would let loose his furious temper on anyone who talked about the females in his family.

He would not be hurried into arranging a marriage for Maraliya. When a girl was being given in marriage, even though she would remain with her mother and father, people asked to which town or village she was being "given," meaning where her bridegroom was from. What he did for a living was secondary to that piece of information. If someone were to ask about his niece, "where are they giving her to?" Wappah wanted to say, more than anything else in the world, *to the Fort*.

When the telephone call that was to change our lives came, we had just moved into a new house in Colombo, a few weeks before my eighteenth birthday. More and more Muslims from the Galle Fort were moving to the capital city for the educational and business opportunities it provided, and we followed suit. Our phone was not yet installed and when one of our neighbors came to say that someone was asking to speak to Wappah, he hurried away. When he returned, he was walking very slowly, his arms stiffly by his sides. Umma went up to speak to him but he held his hand up. We watched without speaking: Umma against the far wall, her hand resting on a doorframe, and me behind my bedroom curtain which I had moved aside. Wappah walked to a chair and sat down. His lips were set tight. He did not speak for many minutes, and it seemed to me that his dark face had got even darker.

Maraliya had run away. With a neighbor, a married man with a wife still living, the father of many children, the youngest still a baby. There was no other information. And none really mattered. What did it signify where they had gone, or when, or how? My father's niece, a komaru, nearly a daughter to him, was now alone with a man who was not her husband. And soon, the whole world would know.

Wappah had built her a house, put away money for her dowry, made diamond jewelry, and ordered a double bed for the wedding chamber that would be set up when a bridegroom was found, which he didn't think would be far in the future. The bed was even now at Marmee's home, smelling of fresh varnish. The shiny sarees, the matching underskirts and slippers, they had all been collected. But nothing had yet worked out. Though they had looked for a bridegroom since she turned sixteen, and the families of some prospective grooms had come by to look, Wappah and Marmee had not found someone, at least not someone they really wanted. At twenty-three, she was already a little old to be unmarried.

Perhaps Maraliya was tired of waiting; perhaps she was bored, spending day after listless day at home from age twelve, when they pulled her out of school. Perhaps she thought they would never find someone for her. Perhaps she didn't mean to do this—it was a harmless flirtation gone wrong. Perhaps she had already gone too far—the man lived right behind their house in the village, behind a fence of dried coconut fronds that gave cover in the dark—and there was no turning back.

When she ran away, Marmee's family had just moved from Shollai into our old house on Lighthouse Street, vacant now because we had come to Colombo. Wappah had wanted her to live there. His sister probably wanted that too. But Maraliya had not been happy. This eldest daughter, who had left behind all her friends, had become desperate. Perhaps she thought such losses too high a price to pay to become a "Fort Family."

Had Marmee suspected? What had she been doing, people asked, allowing such a thing to go on under her very nose? How could she not have known what her daughter was up to, a daughter who lived in the same house? That's what Wappah must have wanted to know too, during the somber hours he spent in the backseat of our car, going by himself with just the driver—he had mutely asked to be alone—to our old house in the Fort.

As the car reached Galle and drove past the esplanade, Wappah would have had a full view of the entrance to the fortress he had first seen as a twelve-year-old child, barefooted, on his way to his first job.

This forbidding stone garrison was made even more impenetrable when, in the 17th century, the Dutch wrested it away from the Portuguese. Over the original mounds of clay and timber were put up stone walls a hundred feet thick; the ramparts were raised to be three times as high. The fortress was now almost impregnable, for besides these gigantic fortifications, where land met sea, were the treacherous currents that swirled in the shallows. Lurking under the water, waiting for the unsuspecting seafarer, were massive granite boulders. Paradoxically, though the harbor of Galle gave shelter, the entrance to it was so perilous that ships never approached unless guided by a pilot dhoni that navigated between reef walls, sandbars and submerged cliffs. The ocean floor was littered, they said, with the shipwrecks of those who had tried to breach the defenses of the Fort.

About a year ago, when I was at her house, Marmee had suddenly come up to where we girls were seated and raised her voice in a way that was unusual for her.

"In those days," she said, breathing fast, "when my mother had to go out, she locked me inside the house. I stayed until she came back; never stepped outside. That's how we were, the komarus of those days."

"Do you see that fence?" she pointed to the barricade of thatched coconut leaves that screened the back garden. "I didn't step outside that by myself, ever. Not during the day, not at night."

Marmee paced up and down. My cousins were squatted over a gunnysack, picking out gravel and stones from a mound of raw rice. Her eyes rested on them for a few moments. Then, she turned around to face me.

"Now, maidens walk into the front verandah during the day. They go by themselves to neighbors' houses. They keep their heads uncovered. They are not obedient." Her voice trembled.

I searched her face. Was she talking to me? Did she think I was not being a good girl? Though I had nothing specific to hide, I always felt a vague sense, as I suspect all young girls did, of being "found out." For who could live up to the purity demanded of us? We were supposed to pretend that we were too innocent to think of anything even remotely connected to boys or men. Not even at family weddings were we to imagine a possible marriage for ourselves. The boys who walked by our houses were not to arouse any more interest than the goats and cows that roamed the streets. The most modest of us, when our own weddings were being planned, had to pretend we knew nothing about it.

Under such conditions, having a romantic interest or being the object of one didn't occur easily. When that did occasionally happen, it was to girls like Rehana and Shenaza, who were the prettiest among us—boys having caught glimpses of them here and there.

Muslim friends like these, who had been my childhood playmates too, became the regular companions of my adolescent years after Penny faded from my life. We spent our time together at family functions, tried to persuade a willing adult to chaperone us to the rare film show, or finagled a nighttime walk along the ramparts. At each other's homes, we engaged in activities considered appropriate for young girls, though here, I was more onlooker than participant. No one ever asked *me* to help embroider a saree blouse, or decorate a cake or help sweep their hair up into a beehive hairdo. But I was good for listening to their stories about scoldings they got from their mothers or fights they had with their siblings, or that most interesting subject of all, which boy was "interested" in which girl.

However different we were, regarding talent and interests, we were all the same in what would have been considered the most important characteristic of all: we were all girls in "hiding."

The Tamil word, *ollikkiya,* for what a maiden was supposed to do to safeguard her modesty, literally meant "to hide." When elders proclaimed the modesty of previous generations, they recounted how much they had *hidden*: from the postman who came to their front door, the strange males who lingered on their verandahs, even the more distant cousins who walked into a front hall. *We hid so much!* Such were the proclamations of the virtuous.

The komarus of my generation hid too; though in more ways than the elders suspected. We hid the Mills & Boon romance novels and *Boyfriend* magazines that were surreptitiously passed around. We talked in low voices about which boys had followed which girls on their bicycles that day; who had stood at a corner to catch a glimpse of whom; and whose concealed handwritten note, *gasp*, had found its way to the intended girl.

Had my aunt found this out? The thought occurred to me, that the romance novels I devoured had front covers that showed a man and a woman in a close embrace. Even someone who didn't know English, like Marmee, could guess their content. Had she suspected something? If she had, I would have liked to tell her that those were just books I read. I no more thought of meeting a boy at the soda fountain, if there were soda fountains in Ceylon, than I thought of being Cinderella or Sleeping Beauty. Which was true also for my friends who were hiding their romantic interests from the elders. They were reveling in a fantasy they had no plans of enacting in real life. At least, that was the case for most komarus, before the wall of seclusion that stood between a young girl and the world outside began to weaken and crack in ways it had never done before.

So what was Marmee trying to say as she walked over to the rice grains, picked up a stone between her jagged fingernails, and threw it out into the garden? With her lips shut tight, she walked up and down and turned around again to face me.

"When that Sithy from your Galle Fort, ran away with a kafir man, her father stopped going to functions, her mother took to her bed, never went out of the house. Her family was finished. How can you show your face to anyone after that?"

Suddenly, we heard Wappah come up the steps from the back garden and Marmee stopped speaking. My cousins lowered their heads and pretended to be wholly absorbed in searching for stones in the rice. Marmee adjusted a fold of her saree and walked away into the kitchen.

Before she did, she fixed her eyes for a second or two on Maraliya.

❀ ❀ ❀

When Wappah, after his grueling journey, arrived in Galle, he found Marmee curled on her bed, her knees brought up to her chest, rocking and moaning. Aunt Asiyatha sat on the floor beside her, stroking her feet. Neither one got up when Wappah entered the room.

"Your father," Aunt Asiyatha told me, many years later when it had become possible for us to speak of that terrible time, "yelled nonstop for hours. He paced up and down the house, yelled, and paced again. He wanted us to get up, to speak to him, to explain how this could have happened. Your Marmee moaned and pleaded for someone to recite hymns to comfort her. Finally, she staggered into the kitchen."

"Your Wappah, he raised his hand, then put it down. That was the first time I ever saw him do that in his life."

18

*No man is alone with a woman
but Satan will be the third one present.*

– Hadith, Tirmidhi

Sithy was a 'fallen woman.' Long before I could know anything about it, she had eloped with her brother's tutor. The men in her family chased them down and dragged them back. The man, they beat up. He was never to set foot anywhere near the Fort again, if he valued his life. Sithy, they locked in a room for days and months and then married off to someone too badly in need of money to refuse the dowry they offered. Some years later, Sithy divorced him and came back to her mother's house.

When Sithy was in the room, mothers sidled up to their daughters and kept close watch. She laughed out loud, showing red lips and brown teeth. Instead of wearing her saree modestly drawn down and secured in front, like other Muslim women, she wore it in the infidel fashion, its free end thrown loosely across a shoulder. She had cut her hair short. When she cupped her hands to light a cigarette, the elders tightened their jaws.

"Do you want to play a game of Donkey Bridge?" she would ask as she took out a deck of cards from inside her blouse.

"No, there's no time for games now, we have to go," the mothers said before turning away to mutter, "What kind of entertainment is *that* for females?"

If someone planned an outing—a picnic, a river bath, a fete in a grand mosque—and Sithy said, "Can I come too?" people pretended they had not heard her.

She was never asked to chaperone a maiden anywhere.

Once, Cousin Fahima Thatha, attracted by Sithy's laughter, had walked the back alleys and snuck into her house. Her father, when he found out, exploded. "He slapped me right across the face and said he would tie me to the bedpost if I ever spent time with Sithy again."

Before she ran away, Sithy had taken to sauntering into the front rooms of her home during the day, which habit seemed not outrageous anymore, considering that many girls stepped out in broad daylight to get into the buggy carts and cars that took them to school. One day, when with her gauzy veil flowing from her shoulders she came out of the inner rooms, she found her brother's tuition master seated at the dining room table. Sithy drew back behind the printed chintz curtains secluding the women's quarters, but not before she noticed that his eyes were fixed on her, and not before he observed that her lower eyelids were lined in gleaming black kohl.

Soon, Sithy timed her need to do something in the front bedroom around the tutor's arrival. She listened to the sound of the afternoon traffic: cart men swishing their canes in the air as they cursed and prodded a reluctant bull, "Go, you dumb jackass!" peddlers calling out their wares, the wooden clogs worn by Arabic scholars going *click, clack, click* on the tarred road. Cars whizzed by and rickshaws rattled over potholes. And in the distance rang the tuition master's bicycle bell as he weaved through the traffic. Lately, it seemed, he rang the bell more loudly as he approached Sithy's house. She positioned herself behind a window that looked out into the street and drew back the curtain. The tutor took his time leaning his bike against the parapet wall, setting the kickstand into place, and locking it up.

"Can we not meet?" he pleaded in the third note he passed to Sithy through the housemaid, who began to get gifts of talcum powder and glass bangles from her young mistress. The housemaid said that could be arranged: in the alleyway, behind the back door, under cover of night. If anyone asked, that was just Sithy going to the outhouse. It was at night too, that Sithy ran away with her lover, leaving her father and mother, her two sisters and brother, and all the families in the Galle Fort to discover with a shudder the next morning that one of their own girls had run away.

Don't ever do this to your family. Don't ever let anything like this happen again, mothers, grandmothers and aunts mutely pleaded as they looked into their daughters' eyes.

For some time, it didn't. Then it happened, again. And again.

It took only minutes for a girl attending the Convent School to get down from a buggy cart and walk into the classrooms. Yet, in that time, she could manage to look from under lowered lashes at the boy from the Jesuit College nearby who had fixed his gaze on her. He waited every morning until she arrived. She rewarded his patience with a clandestine glance; each longed for the same thing to happen the next day. Christian schoolmates giggled and offered to pass love notes. Phone calls were made. "I am going to have a l-o-n-g chat with cousin Ameera," a girl announced to her family before dialing *his* number.

Without much face-to-face conversation, without a holding of hands or brushing of lips, girls and boys pledged understanding. The chaperones swore they had been vigilant all the time. "How could this happen under our very noses?" they asked.

Furious families yanked their daughters out of school and married them off to a "suitable boy." Sometimes, the girl gave up the romance on her own, terrified to be treated like Sithy, unwilling to be the downfall of her family. Sometimes, gossamer feelings fed purely on long looks and shy smiles waned on their own. When there was a lull, people calmed down. Then, first one girl and then another did the unspeakable thing and eloped.

The community had to relearn what their forebears must have known when they set the rules for female seclusion. Passion fed on miniscule fare: heart-catching tendrils breaking loose from under a veil, muscles tensing against a thin cotton shirt, and desire seized the heart. Black robes draped from head to toe gave some protection. Confining women entirely to the inner rooms mostly worked. Lesser safeguards, it was turning out, were lines drawn in the sand.

19

All things of a Muslim are sacred for his brother-in-faith: his blood, his property, and his honor.

– The Prophet's Farewell Sermon

Wappah stopped going out of the house except to his shop. He spent hours on his recliner, looking into the distance. He walked away from people, and if someone spoke, responded with tight-lipped silence or a curt word. Umma asked most visitors to keep away. We were quiet when he was around.

When, about two months after Maraliya's running away, our neighbor and relative Omar Kaka invited Umma and me to go along with his family to the hillside resort town of Nuwara Eliya, we eagerly accepted. It would be a break from the sadness that enveloped everything. Wappah seemed glad to have us outside the house.

On our third day at Nuwara Eliya, the phone rang for Umma. The connection being poor, she couldn't make out exactly what had happened, but we were asked to come home immediately, there was a crisis of some kind. My Uncle Shinnamama was on his way to bring us back.

On the car ride, we got bits and pieces of information. Wappah had beaten the man who ran off with Maraliya. The man had come to our house in Colombo. No one was sure why: whether he came on his own or whether Wappah had lured him there. After the runaway couple had been discovered, Maraliya had been forcibly taken away by her brother and entrusted to a relative who lived some distance away. Now the man wanted her returned. He wanted to marry her. He was a Muslim and could have a second wife.

"When your father saw him, he screamed and lunged," Cader Machan, Maraliya's brother, reported to us.

"Your father," my cousin continued, "hit the man with whatever he could get hold of. The neighbors heard the noise and called the police. They took him to hospital and your father to jail. They arrested me too, because I was there, then they let me go."

Two days later, the man, who was recovering from TB, died.

Sheriff Nana, who was the first to hear this, fainted when he got the news.

Had Wappah's rage got the better of him? Had he planned such a thing all along? The man had come by that day, he said, to get Maraliya back. Had he been asked to come? Cader Machan gave a vague reply. That could have been. He wasn't certain. Wappah was unwilling to talk, his nephew unwilling to say anything against his uncle. And the rest of us, devastated by the tragedy for the widow and her fatherless children, could not bring ourselves to comment or question. In police custody now, all my father would say was, "He deserved it. He rubbed soot on our faces."

You could smell Welikada remand jail before you saw it. The reek of urine from the open drains where men relieved themselves wafted all the way down to the turn from the main road. It became stronger as we drove up to the Superintendent's office where I was going to see Wappah.

For weeks, Umma had wrestled with the question of how I was going to see him. I could not enter the visiting hall of a prison. My being in a room with strange men; Wappah would not allow that—not even to see him.

Finally, a relative who knew a government official arranged a private meeting—just Umma and Wappah and me in the superintendent's office.

I waited. My head veiled. My eyes fixed on the doorway.

I first saw Wappah in the hallway, walking slowly, a tin plate in his hand—he would use it to take back to his cell the food we brought. His once round face was thin and drawn. His cheeks were speckled with grey stubble and the undershirt he wore sloped off one shoulder. I stood up from my chair and moved forward. Wappah stumbled at the threshold.

We put our arms around each other, his tears falling on my shoulder and mine dampening the top of his undershirt. Finally, he said something. Through the years, he'd had many names for me: *rajathi*, princess, *manikkam*, jewel, and *kalla kutti*, naughty little girl. He used none of these now. He called me by a word he had never used before— *mahal*—daughter.

As I held on to my father, I remembered nothing of the harsh words that were being said about him; words relayed to us by people who visited just for that purpose—to fulfill their duty, they probably convinced themselves, to let us know.

He didn't pray five times a day.

He never listened to anyone, else someone could have warned him about his niece.

Didn't he stop to think about that family, so many children without a father?

Why didn't he punish her, the one who ran away?

Allah had obviously singled him out for punishment.

Saida Marmee stopped by to tell Umma, "This will affect your daughter most of all. When it comes time for marriage, when people ask about the family..." she shook her head.

In a jail cell with no windows, Wappah slept on a straw mat on the cement floor. At home, he had slept on a bed custom-built by Don Carolis and Sons, the finest furniture maker in the country. It was so large, it couldn't be taken through the doorway of the small flat we had lived in for a few months before we moved to our house in Colombo.

But Wappah said nothing about the windowless cell, or straw mat on the floor, or the smell of urine in the air. He held the back of a chair, and with his eyes welling, looked up at the Superintendent. "Please, sir," pleaded my father, who had worked since he was twelve years old. "I cannot bear to be idle. Give me something to do. Anything at all."

20

And among His signs is this, that He created for you mates from among yourselves that you may dwell in tranquility with them.

– The Quran, 30: 21

ine months later, Wappah came home on bail. And went back to a behavior he had acquired since the day Maraliya ran away. He needed to know, almost every minute of the day, where exactly I was.

I heard the panic in his voice.

"Where is she? Where's the child?"

"She's in the bathroom."

"Are you certain?"

"Yes, she's in there."

"Go look. Knock on the door. Make sure."

His face visibly relaxed when I appeared.

The conversation among Umma's cousins who gathered for afternoon tea focused more and more on how "girls have become different."

"We began to go out of the house," Kaneema Marmee said, recollecting the changes that had taken place since she was a girl in the early 1900s. "We went to the bazaar and did our shopping from the buggy carts; then we went right into the shops. Some women took the bus to Colombo too, though there were strange men sitting next to them; they were shy at first, but they got used to it.

"When our own Macan Markar from the Galle Fort ran for State Council, in the 1930s, he needed the votes. The Ulemas at the Grand Mosque in Colombo said: *Women should not vote: it is the duty of men not to allow women to plunge into unavoidable anxieties.* But he got them to change their mind. We were driven in curtained cars to the polling stations."

"Then all that going to school, some girls even went to work, and became teachers..." Zubeida Marmee chewed on her wad of betel leaves and mused.

"They have become too independent; they don't listen to their mothers and fathers. Not even their husbands."

Some girls who were "going out of the house," and even some who were not, were no longer willing, it seemed, to marry anyone their parents chose, or if they did, to stay with him until the very end. Even men who were considered to be good husbands from good families.

Noorul Ayne Aunty, when she heard of a broken engagement initiated, unimaginably, by the girl, asked: if there was no drinking, or gambling, or other women, or money problems, why does she not want to marry him? "She says they are not... not comp... compat... what's that English word?"

"Compatible?" someone suggested.

"Yes, that's the one. What does that mean?"

"It means they have to be suitable for each other."

"But they are! We don't arrange marriages with unsuitable people!"

"It means the girl and the boy, they have to feel like they want the same things."

"Don't husbands and wives want the same things?"

"They do, but they say they have to have things in common as well."

"They are Muslims! Isn't that enough in common?"

Elders set their eyes intently and anxiously on young faces. *Is there something we should know, but don't?* They couldn't keep their daughters out of school entirely, when all girls now got at least some education. No young person was willing to spend all her days in the inner rooms of the house anymore. Some families married their daughters off as soon as they could. Others held their breath and hoped that those who were going out would return home no different than they had been.

But that didn't always happen. The words *girl, likes,* and *him* were used more and more in the same sentence.

And the "him" grief-stricken relatives were forced to accept was sometimes a pork-eating, uncircumcised infidel.

"So I told my brother, when I heard the news" — Fatheela Marmee was talking about her niece— "what kind of nonsense is this? What does she mean, she only wants to marry him, and nobody else? Is he the only doctor in the world? We'll find her a Muslim doctor, if a doctor is what she wants. We can do that."

"But my brother tells me she does not want to marry anyone else, only him. I never heard of such a thing. There is only one person in the world she will marry? I told him to ask her, I did, I was so angry, I told him, ask her, 'why does it have to be him and only him? Is his thing made of gold? Is that why?'"

There had been a time when the Muslim women in the country were supposed to die before they allowed a kafir to touch them. When, in 1915, riots broke out in Ceylon, and the Sinhalese attacked the vastly outnumbered Muslims, rumors of murder and rape terrified the community. The Ulemas in the Grand Mosque in Colombo sent out a ruling: *The men will fight to the last, but if the tide turns against them, the women, rather than being ravished, will jump into the wells and commit suicide.*

"When my sister ran away with the bricklayer who had been building the house next door," Raheema Thatha said, "my mother sat on her bed, speechless, her eyes wide. Her teeth chattered and her whole body shook for hours. I held her for a long time. She never recovered from the shock of that."

Other relatives had similar stories. "My brother, Rahim, he set fire to everything that had belonged to his daughter: clothes, books, shoes, and photographs. Refuses to speak her name."

"My cousin, Haseena, rolled on the floor and cried. Would not eat for days. Maybe that's why she got cancer and died a year later."

The Ulemas spoke of *fitna*, Arabic for *chaos, affliction, distress, temptation, trial, sedition,* and the community was reminded of a fundamental principle in the religion: when something is prohibited, anything which leads to it is prohibited too. Alluring clothes, seductive music, lewd images, private meetings, most of all, women going out of the house—they could all lead to what was the ultimate forbidden act: an amorous relationship outside of marriage.

Perhaps that's why, generations later, the heavy covering of the abaya, with only an opening for eyes, came back. A shield between a girl and her surroundings, it allowed a maiden to be separated from the world, and her family to believe that she was just as secluded as her grandmother had been, who never stepped out of the house.

The elders did not speak of the less visible but more potent gateways to fitna. Pathways that could not be blocked off with thick black cloth, because they occurred inside the minds of girls exposed to foreign ideas. The conflict that might occur in a young person trying to reconcile the values of obedience and freedom, the welfare of the family and the rights of one person; ideas that sometimes made a maiden want something other than what her parents planned for her.

I heard no elder pondering the question of how to reconcile the benefits of modernity with the traditions that nurtured stable families. No one asked what the cost might have been for girls, of such severe confinement and seclusion as sought to guard them. Whether the listless days of the "fallen girls" could have been the very thing that had pushed them to make those disastrous choices.

Grandaunt Saadeth Marmee was speaking for her generation when she described what she believed was the root of all these problems. "Men and women," she said, "are like cotton-wool and fire. Only the heedless let them get near each other."

27

He who wishes to enter paradise at the best gate
must please his father and mother.

– Hadith, Bukhari

Umma and Wappah didn't think, when they let me stay in school to take the twelfth grade university entrance examinations, that this had anything to do with my going there. In the years after eight grade, when I felt the first stirrings of the desire to further my education beyond secondary school, I told no one about it.

When Rameesa Marmee asked whether I would be leaving home, Umma said, "Goodness, no. She likes school, so we just allowed her to stay a little longer."

Wappah was surprised that I wanted anything beyond what he considered the pinnacle of a person's education: the Senior School Certificate, awarded after the tenth grade. Most of the clerks in government offices who lorded it over him had that revered qualification, and he couldn't

imagine anything more awe-inspiring. But in the
end he said, "Alright, alright, you can stay two
more years, if you want to."

Some months after Wappah had come home on
bail, I was admitted to the University of Ceylon
in Peradeniya, a residential campus seventy-two
miles away.

When I told Umma that I had been accepted
and wanted to go there, she widened her eyes.

"I'm going to ask Wappah."

"I don't know…I don't know if you should do
that." Umma shook her head.

But, I did.

"What?" Wappah sat up from his reclining chair
where he had been smoking his cigar. "Where do
you want to go?"

"To the university."

Wappah hollered. "Alavia!"

Umma came running. All through her married
life, she had heard Wappah hollering and it rarely
made her walk any faster than in her usually
sedate style. But this, it must have seemed to her,
was something different.

"Do you know anything about this?"

"About what?"

"Her going to this place."

Umma bit her lip and looked at me. "What is
your father talking about?"

"That's exactly what I want to know." Wappah
could barely stand still. "What is *she* talking
about?"

"I don't know. I don't know." Umma would not meet his eyes. She kept wringing her hands.

In the days that followed, we covered the same ground.

"Are you out of your...what are you thinking of...who put this idea into your..."

"All I'll do is study. I'll stay on the campus. I won't go anywhere else."

"You'll be away from home. By yourself, among unknown people."

"But I really would like to go."

"What does it matter what you would like to do? Has anyone heard of a komaru doing such a thing?"

"It's the only thing I want."

Wappah tossed his cigar aside and walked away.

Wappah's voice resounded from the front bedroom. "What kind of disgrace is this? Alone, by herself with strange men, who imagines this for a young girl?"

What Umma said in reply, I couldn't always make out.

"Has any girl in *your* family gone away like this? *Your* family is the first to imitate the Parangis. If no one else in *your* family has done that, why should she?"

There were long silences before Wappah's voice thundered again.

"I used to have her lie down in the car when we drove through the Galle bazaar. That's how carefully I protected her."

This was true. I lay down in the backseat of our un-curtained car when we rode through the main commercial areas of Galle. Many Muslim families at the time had cars that were screened with an expanse of cloth curtaining the backseat from the front, and the side windows from the road. But not us. There being three boys, it would mean that, on family trips, one of them would be seated behind, secluded, which my brothers would not even consider. Wappah reconciled himself to my being driven about "in the open," as he called it, within the Galle Fort and to school (though he did encourage me to sit as inconspicuously as possible in a corner), but he would not allow his daughter to be seen by men in the Galle bazaar among whom would be acquaintances from the old village. Fortunately for me, a car with a roomy backseat had come into our family.

"I got the car out for her even to go to that cake lady's house, not ten yards away. So now is she going to be walking about in broad daylight in this Peradeniya place…?"

Rameesa Marmee, who had taken her eldest daughter out of school after the fifth grade and whose heart beat fast when she had to speak to anyone on the phone (that being something so strange to her), came by to talk to me.

She took my hand.

"We are all waiting to see you married. If he made these for your naming ceremony," she pushed back her hair to show the earrings, "imagine what he would make for a wedding."

As she spoke, I fiddled with my chain. I can't remember what I was wearing around my neck that day. My father had made many necklaces for me. It could have been the chain of gold beads or the string of interlocking petals, but it would definitely not have been the row of diamond flowers, each set on tiny springs, which erupted into a frenzied sparkle with the slightest move— my father's own invention which procured for him the admiration of other jewelers.

It had been some time since I didn't feel the need to wear much jewelry or do anything else the elders said *a girl should do*. So as not to disappoint Wappah, I made sure I was wearing something when he was around. But he didn't know about those times when I took the bracelets, chains and earrings off, any more than he knew my real reason for taking a university entrance exam.

Rameesa Marmee looked intently at me without speaking. Perhaps she was wondering whether I was as obedient a girl as she had always thought me. Perhaps she was thinking of Mackiya Thatha who had been educated beyond the attainments of the men in the community and had ended up old and unmarried. Perhaps she wanted to tell me that if I followed the traditions she valued, I would get used to it and eventually be happy. I said nothing.

Wappah kept saying he'd never thought that letting me stay in school would end up with *this*.

What he did not say was: *You think I'll let you out of my sight after what your cousin did?*

For the first time in our lives, we were not speaking to each other. I did not go out front to greet him when he returned from work. And he did not tweak my nose and call me a *kalla kutti*. If we crossed each other in the hallway, we looked straight ahead.

Just once during that time, after he had returned from Friday prayers at the mosque, he sat across from me at the dining table and asked: "And what about my situation? You want to go while my case is still going on? When we don't know what will happen? I might have to go back to jail."

My eyes welled up, but I couldn't bring myself to say anything that would put him at ease.

My application forms arrived and I told Umma I would lose my spot at the university if I did not send them back in time. She put them away in her dresser drawer with her jewelry.

The next day, Umma paced up and down the front hall while Wappah got ready for work, followed him to the front door and waited until the car was out of the driveway. Then she walked to the dining room and picked up the phone.

Speaking in a low voice to Ryta Shachi, another daughter of the Rohani Cassim family who, many years ago, had been one of the first to stay in school after she became a "big girl," she said something about the university. Next, she phoned her lawyer uncle Fallun Shacha.

He came to our house and said he wanted to talk about my going away. Wappah couldn't refuse. He had to respect the request of an older person; besides, this was the lawyer who was helping him with his court case. We met in the front office.

"There's a special boarding hall for girls there," Fallun Shacha said, as he put some tobacco into his pipe and tamped it with a finger.

"She will be living by herself. Who is going to take her around?" Wappah's voice was defiant, though, in Fallun Shacha's presence, not quite as much as it could be.

"She doesn't have to go about much. Only to classes and back."

"Go about?" Wappah tightened his lips.

"A few of our girls from other towns have gone there and come back safely. Things are changing now."

Umma clasped her hands and held them tight.

"And don't forget," Fallun Shacha continued, "Bunchy is at Peradeniya already. We can arrange to have him stay in the hall right next to hers."

Wappah sat up. "You can do that?"

"Well, that is..." Fallun Shacha paused for a few moments. "We can talk to the warden."

"Who's that?"

"You don't know who the warden is? Why, that's the lady they have in every boarding hall, especially to look after the girls. She lives right there with them."

"A married lady?"

"I don't...Yes, yes, married. They are all married."

Wappah looked out into the garden for some time, then brought his gaze back into the room. "People will talk about our sending a komaru away from home. That's not something our people do."

Umma turned to face him.

"It's not as though you've always cared about what people say. You refuse to go behind holy-men and won't vote for the UNP, and don't believe in superstitions."

Wappah turned to me. "Do you promise that you will not do anything you shouldn't?" His eyes were focused intently on my face.

"I promise," I said very quietly.

"Well, then, you can go if you want to; I will give the money. But I won't take you there. I don't want anything more to do with that." He stood up and walked away.

Umma said she would take me to the university, and did.

❄ ❄ ❄

Two months after I had arrived at Peradeniya, my friend Fareeza came running up to me at the library.

I went there anytime I could. Even in the blazing afternoon sun, when everyone else was glad to stay within. My roommate, who was usually settling in for her siesta, laughed when I reached for my parasol. "I don't know why you have to go," she said as she rolled over and brought the covers around her. "It's not like we have a tutorial due."

It was the first time in seven years that I walked in broad daylight alone. The uneasy feeling that something was not right—the same feeling that came up the first time I was shut in, alone, for a tutorial with a male lecturer—was now almost gone. My friends stopped observing that I looked down when I walked, but still commented that I walked outside for no reason at all.

"Your father is at Wijewardene Hall; he has come to see you," Fareeza said after she caught her breath. "I told him you were in the library. He said he would walk up here and look for you in the girls' section. But I told him I'll fetch you."

We both ran back. As we got nearer, I adjusted my veil, drawing it around me as I hardly ever did anymore.

Wappah was seated in the visitor's lobby. On the floor nearby was a full gunnysack. He had, he told me after we had hugged, taken the train from Colombo, and stopped at the Kandy market to buy me the fruits and sweets. "You can share them with your friends," he said as he wiped the sweat from his brow with his large handkerchief.

We sat across from each other and smiled.

"It's not the same in the house. You know how you bring flowers from the garden and put them into bottles of water. You need a young girl for all that, to keep the house nice. We are old people, your Umma and me..." Wappah shook his head.

I nodded.

"And there's no one to fight with me when I have my two half-boiled eggs in the morning."

"You can have two eggs, Wappah, I've told you that. But you must throw out the yolk from one of them. That's where the cholesterol is. The doctor said..."

"Never mind, never mind all that." Wappah reached into the gunnysack and handed me a sapodilla fruit. Then he settled down to peeling one for himself.

"So where do you go for school?"

· I pointed vaguely in the direction of the Arts faculty, about a mile away, where I hoped to do a degree in English—the language that had tripped up my father, and by extension his family. He peered out and thought I meant the Science building right next door. I didn't tell him he was mistaken.

"Ah, good, good," he said. "It's a short walk, you don't have to be on the road for very long."

"Mmmm," I said.

"The lady teachers? How are they?"

"Well, the lady teachers, that is..." I mumbled.

Wappah's eyes were fixed on the sapodilla fruit and his penknife.

"How is the food here?"

"Good!" I said, sitting up in my chair. "The food is very good."

"And you have nice friends?"

"Yes. Very nice friends."

"You are happy then?"

"I am," I smiled.

"Aah. That's good." Wappah bit into his sapodilla fruit. "I like to see you happy."

❀ ❀ ❀

Postscript

The daughters of the Galle Fort, like many Muslim girls in the rest of the country, now stay in school to complete at least a high school education. It is not unusual anymore for them to travel unchaperoned, or go to university, and among them are countless teachers, lawyers, doctors, scientists and accountants.

Paradoxically, while more women have left behind traditional roles, large sections of the community have turned back to conservative, even fundamentalist practices. In the past several years, the once discarded head scarf has become ubiquitous, and the burka that covers a woman from head to toe, which was rarely seen anywhere in the country a generation ago, is everywhere present

The resurgence of austere orthodox practices in the Islamic world, has, no doubt, its roots in complex geo-political issues. But it's hard not to wonder whether such regression is also not, to a large extent, a push back against what is perceived as the evils of modernity. As Muslim women have become more educated and economically independent, they have also adopted new ideas about marriage and family: they are marrying later or not marrying at all; it is no longer unusual for them to marry outside their faith and community, nor to initiate divorce, the rates of which have sky rocketed in Sri Lanka as elsewhere in the Islamic world. Today, as the dual pressures of orthodox Islam and political fervor bear down, parents face the same challenge that came up three generations ago in the Galle Fort, when girls were first allowed to go to school: how to give a daughter her freedom while still upholding the traditions that sustain stable families and close knit community.

❈ ❈ ❈

For those readers who wish to know the fate of my father: he was found guilty and fined but not jailed. In their judgment, the court took into consideration the circumstances under which the terrible deed was committed. In later years, my mother tried to help the wronged family with money, but her efforts were understandably rebuffed. There are some offences for which no compensation can be made, and we have had, sadly, to leave it at that.

NOTE TO THE READER:

This memoir is based on my recollections, and stories told by my family elders. Where their memories or mine have failed, I have taken the liberty of writing in what is most likely to have happened. For dramatic effect, some events and timelines have been compressed and conversations recreated or supplemented. The names and identifying details of certain individuals have been changed to respect their privacy.

Glossary of Relationships

Wappah — Father

Umma — Mother

Wappumma — father's mother

Marmee — my father's only sister. Marmee is the Tamil word for aunt.

Marma — My aunt Marmee's husband. Marma is the Tamil world for uncle.

Asiyatha — father's cousin — the adopted daughter of his mother's only brother.

Rohani Cassim — great-grandfather. My mother's father's father.

Thalha Cassim — eldest daughter of Rohani Cassim. Being the sister of my mother's father, she was my grand-aunt.

Kaneema Marmee — Thalha Cassim's eldest daughter. My mother's first cousin.

Fathuma Aunty — one of Thalha Cassim's younger daughters, sister to Kaneema Marmee.

Zain Marma — One of my mother's maternal uncles. Of all my grandmother's many siblings, my mother was closest to him.

Zain Marmee — Zain Marma's wife whom we affectionately called by her husband's name.

Maraliya, Hidaya and Nabeesa my father's nieces — his only sister's daughters.

Mackiya Thatha — My mother's second cousin. Thatha is an honorific meaning "elder sister."

Rameesa Marmee — the daughter of one of my father's half-brothers. Having married one of my mother's younger brothers, she was both my cousin and aunt by marriage.

Shinnamatha — one of several poor women who made a living in the Galle Fort by cooking food and helping out in the better off families.

Kadija Marmee and Zubeida Marmee — two of my mother's close relatives who regularly visited our home.

Penny — my childhood friend in the Galle Fort. A Christian of Dutch Burgher descent. Her mother and father were Aunty June and Uncle Quintus.

Yasmin Azad was born and raised in the Galle Fort, Sri Lanka. After obtaining a degree in English from the University of Ceylon, and a brief stint as a lecturer, she moved to the United States in her twenties. She recently retired after many years as a mental health counselor.

OTHER BOOKS YOU MAY LIKE BY **PH** PUBLISHERS

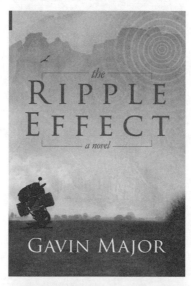

the
RIPPLE
EFFECT
a novel

GAVIN MAJOR

AMEENA
HUSSEIN

THE
MOON
IN THE
WATER

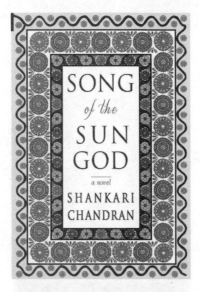

SONG
of the
SUN
GOD
a novel
SHANKARI
CHANDRAN

Nayomi Munaweera

ISLAND *of A*
THOUSAND
MIRRORS
a novel